Masterpieces of

Titian

(1908)

ISBN-13 : 978-1512311075
ISBN-10 : 1512311073

Dtp
and
visual art

Iacob Adrian

THE

MASTERPIECES

OF

TITIAN

Sixty reproductions of photographs from the original paintings, principally by F. Hanfstaengl, affording examples of the different characteristics of the Artist's work

Author statement

This is a series of art books .

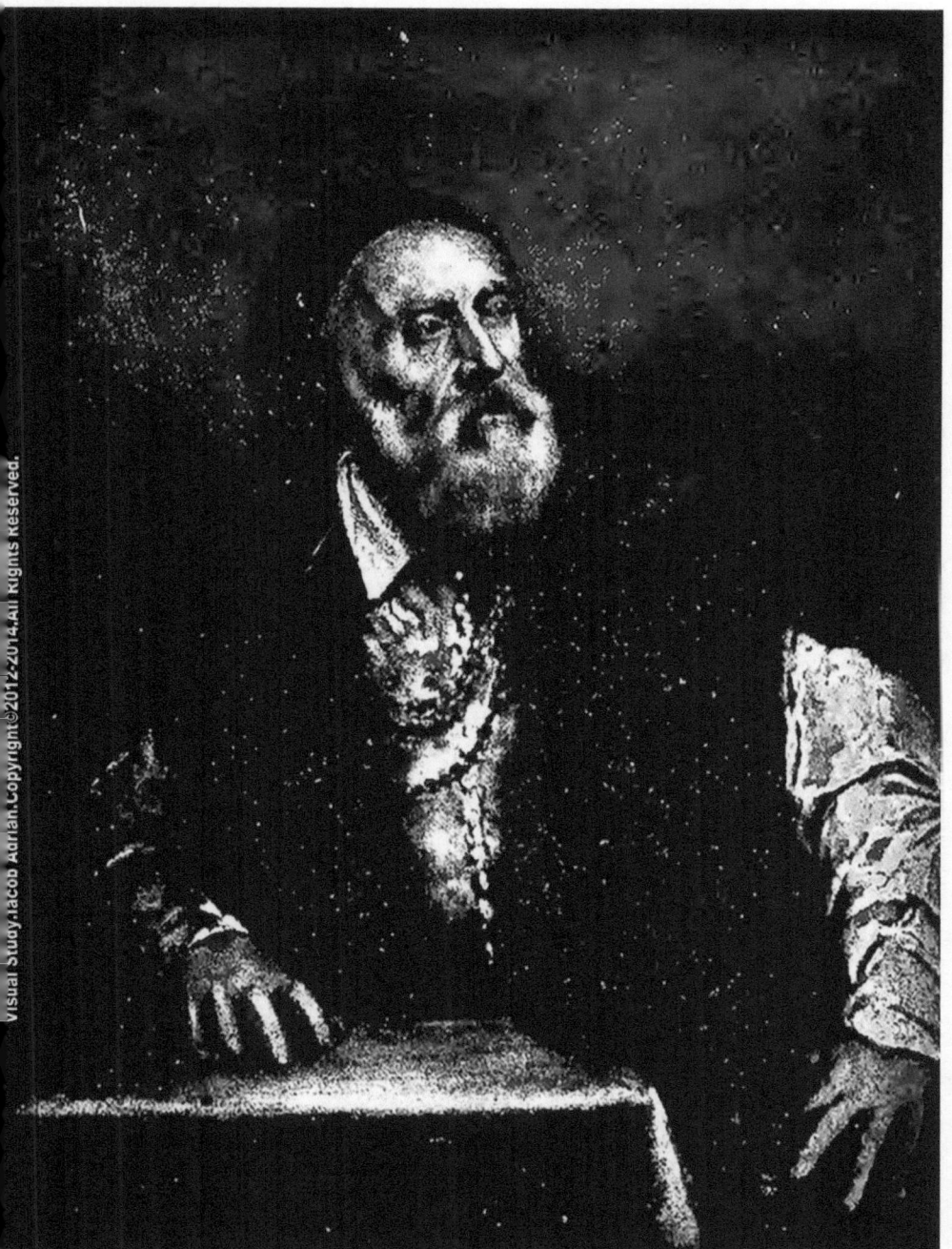

PORTRAIT OF HIMSELF
(*Royal Gallery, Berlin*)

PORTRAIT DE L'ARTISTE
(*Musée royal, Berlin*)

SELBSTBILDNIS
(*Berlin, Kgl. Galerie*)
F. Hanfstaengl, Photo.

This little Book conveys the greetings of

....

to

....

————————————————

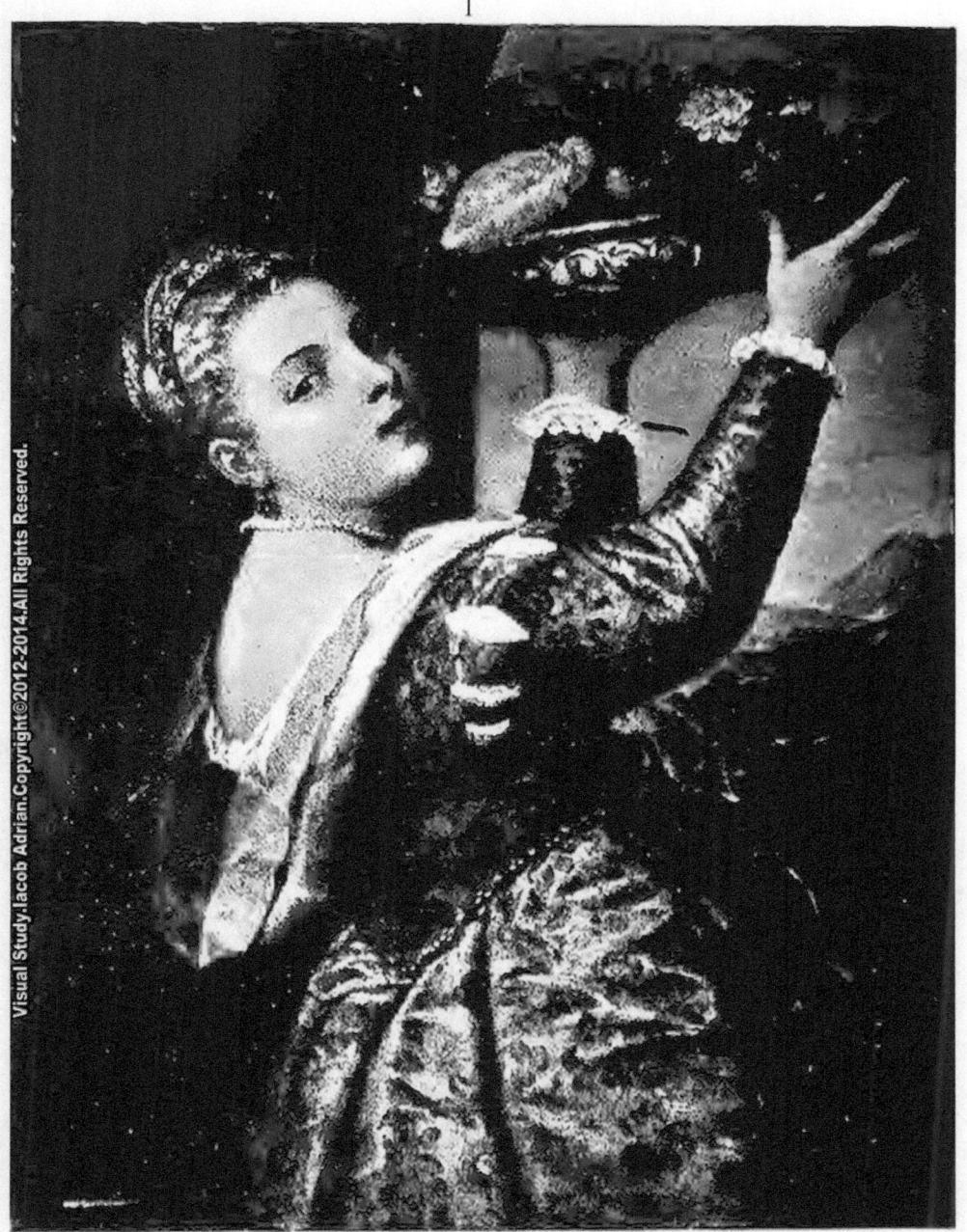

TITIAN'S DAUGHTER, LAVINIA   LAVINIA, FILLE DU TITIEN
(Foyal Gallery, Berlin)   *(Musée royal, Berlin)*
DES KÜNSTLERS TOCHTER LAVINIA
(Berlin, Kgl. Galerie)
F. Hanfstaengl, Photo.

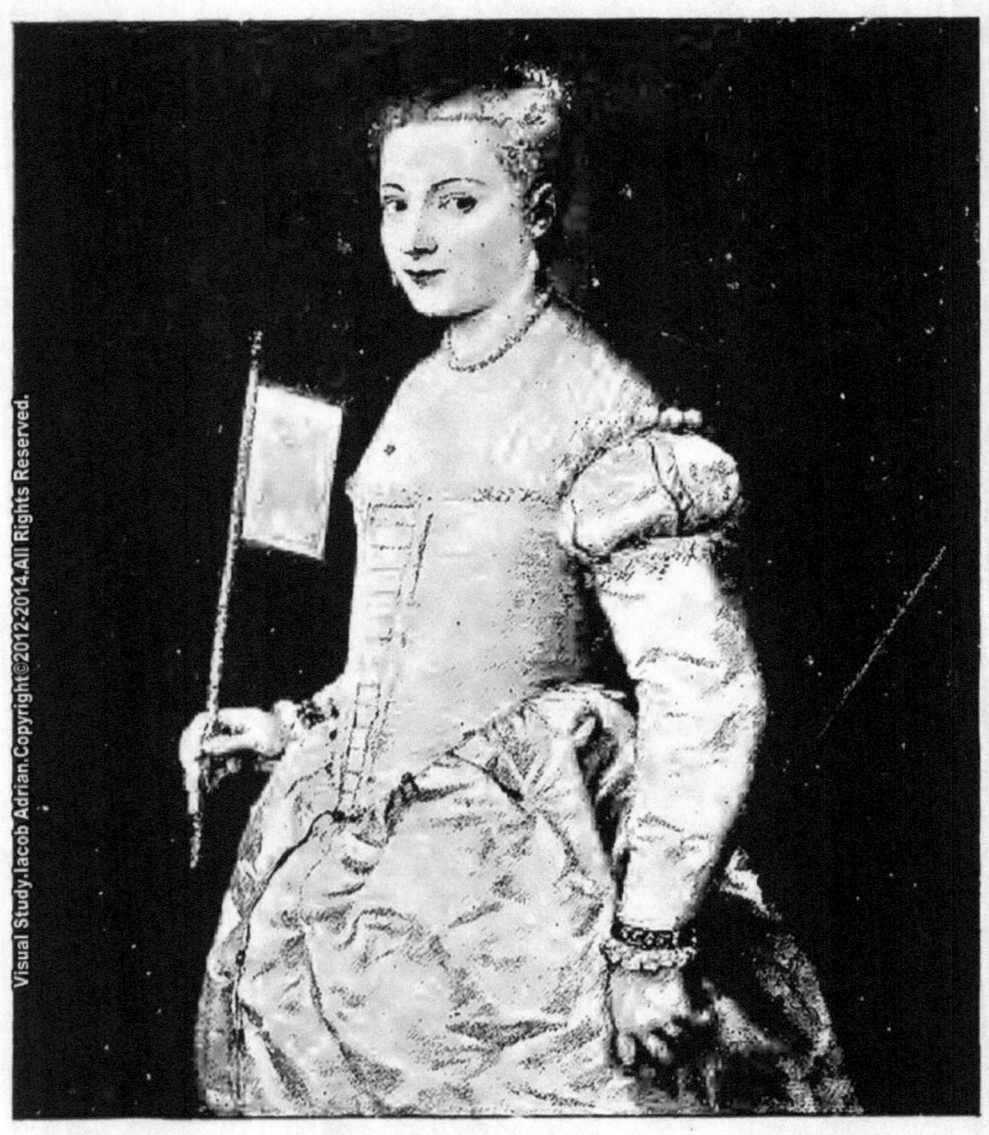

TITIAN'S DAUGHTER, LAVINIA,
AS A BRIDE
(*Royal Gallery, Dresden*)

LAVINIA, EN JEUNE
MARIÉE
(*Galerie royale, Dresde*)

TIZIANS TOCHTER LAVINIA ALS NEUVERMÄHLTE
(*Dresden, Kgl. Galerie*)
F. Hanfstaengl, Photo.

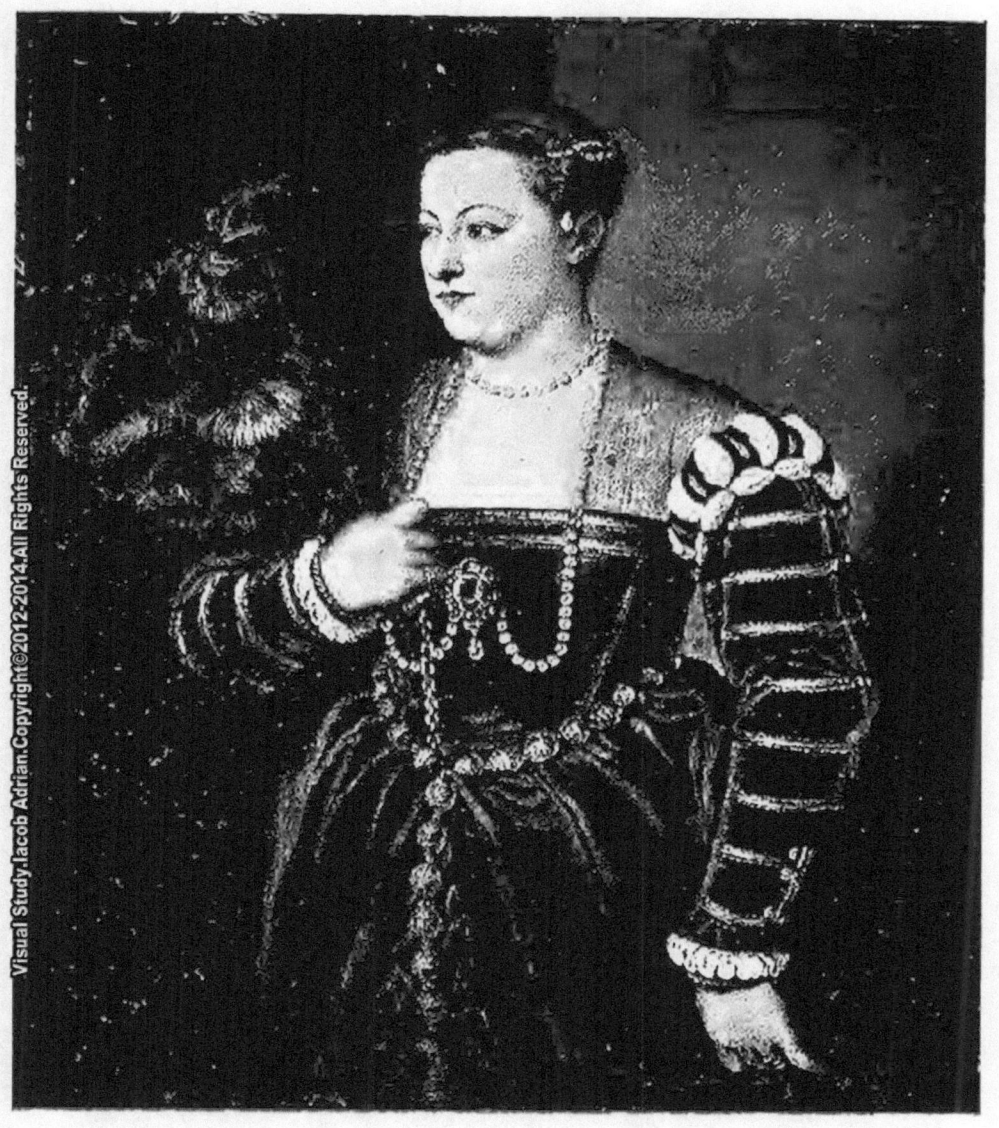

TITIAN'S DAUGHTER, LAVINIA, AS A
MARRIED WOMAN
(*Royal Gallery, Dresden*)

LAVINIA, EN FEMME
(*Galerie royale, Dresde*)

TIZIANS TOCHTER LAVINIA ALS FRAU
(*Dresden, Kgl. Galerie*)
F. Hanfstaengl, Photo.

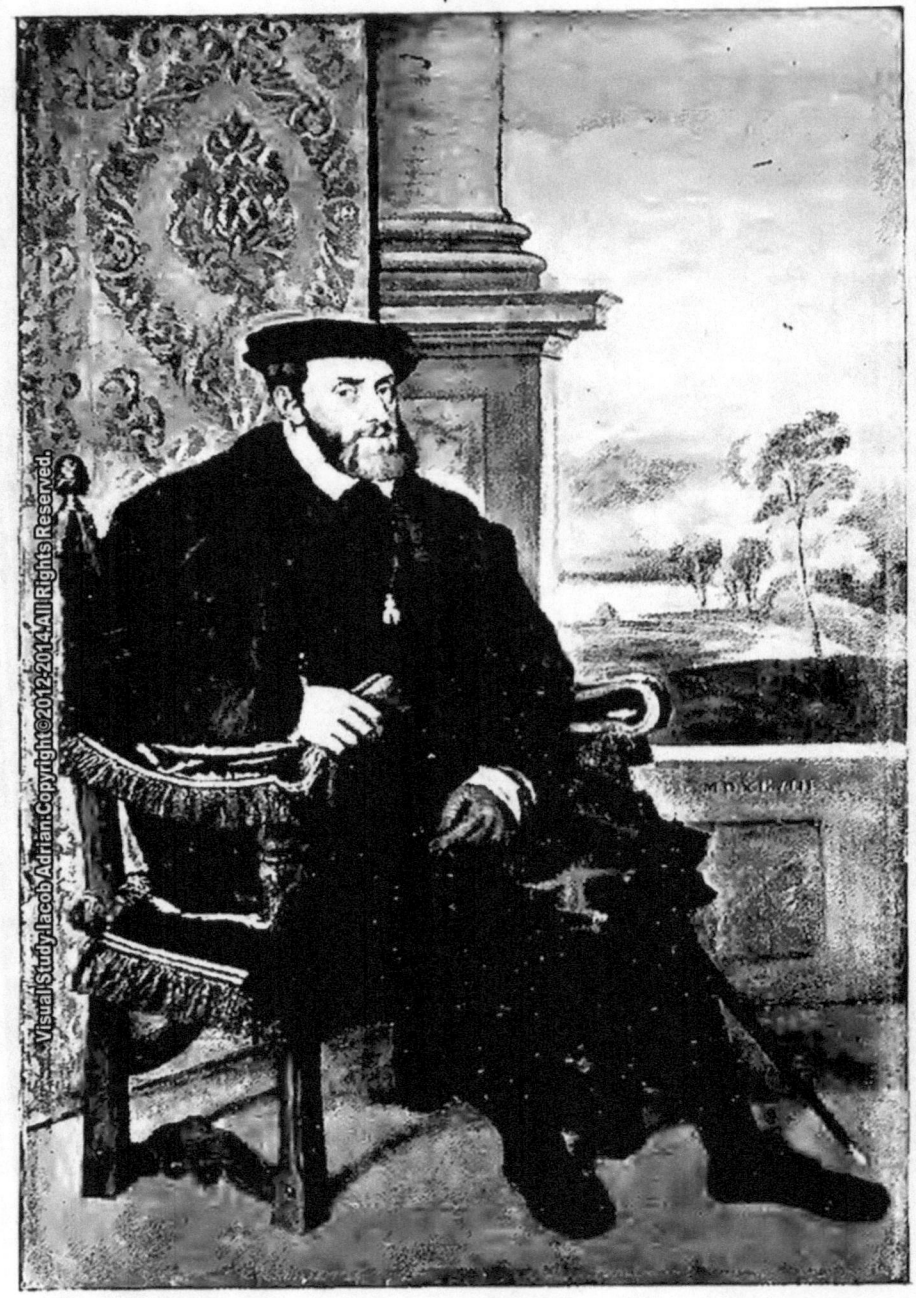

EMPEROR CHARLES V.
(Pinakothek, Munich)

L'EMPEREUR CHARLES-QUINT
(Pinacothèque, Munich)

KAISER KARL V.
(München, Pinakothek)
F. Hanfstaengl, Photo.

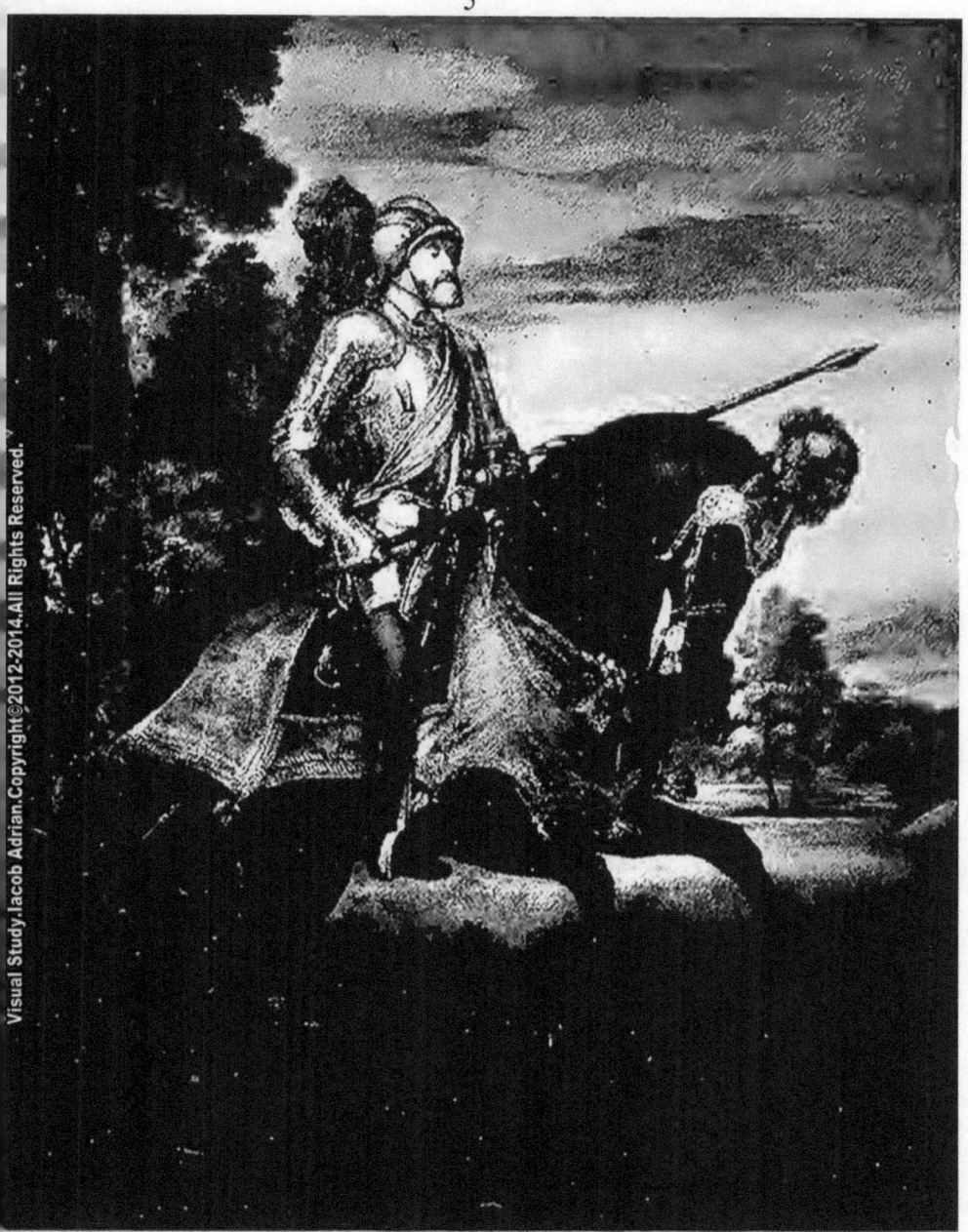

CHARLES V. AT MÜHLBERG   CHARLES-QUINT A MÜHLBERG
(*Prado, Madrid*)   (*Prado, Madrid*)
KARL V. BEI MÜHLBERG
(*Madrid*, Prado)
Braun, Clément & Co., Photo.

6

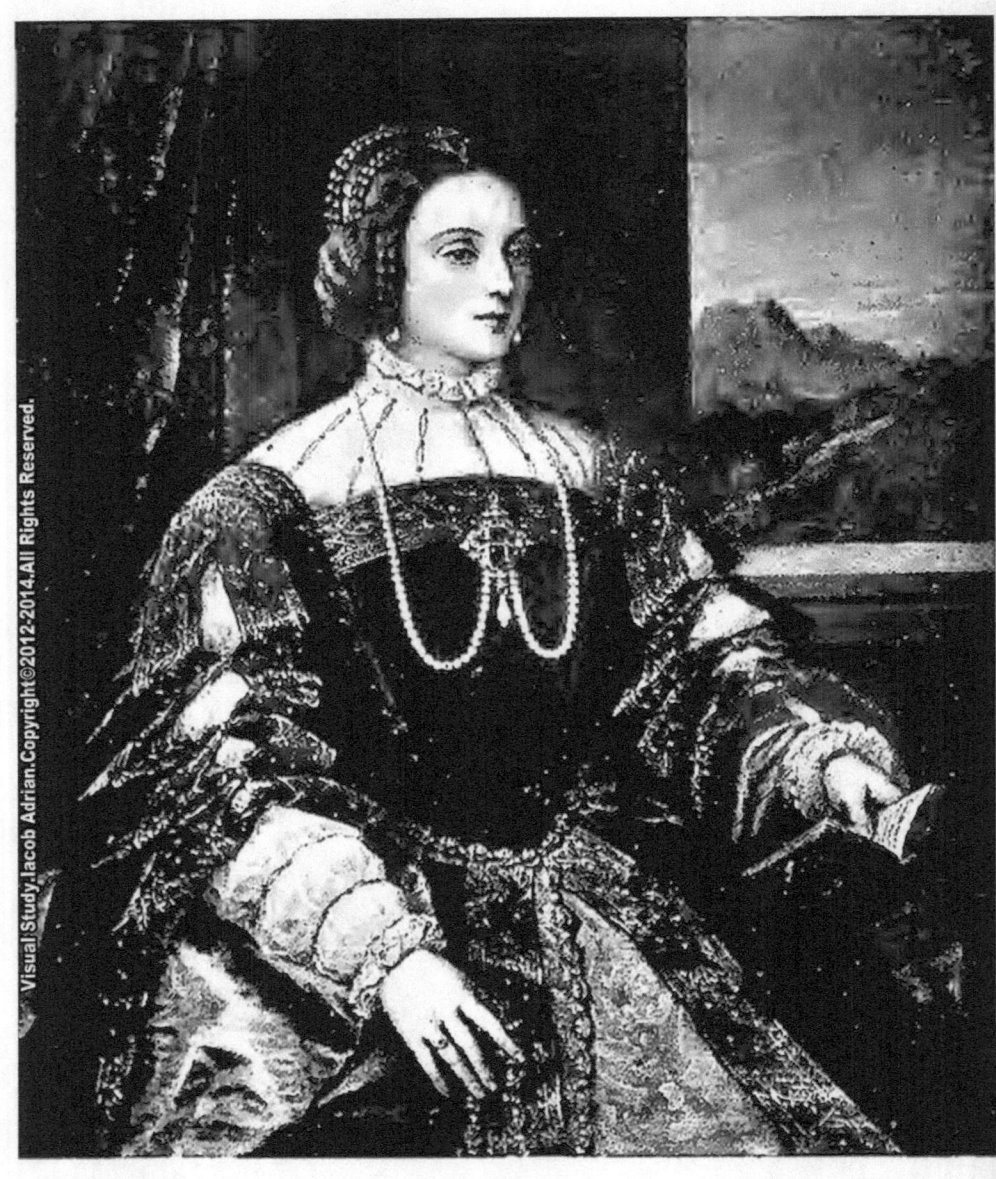

ISABELLA OF PORTUGAL   ISABELLE DE PORTUGAL
(*Prado, Madrid*)   (*Prado, Madrid*)
ISABELLA VON PORTUGAL
(*Madrid, Prado*)
Braun, Clément & Co., Photo.

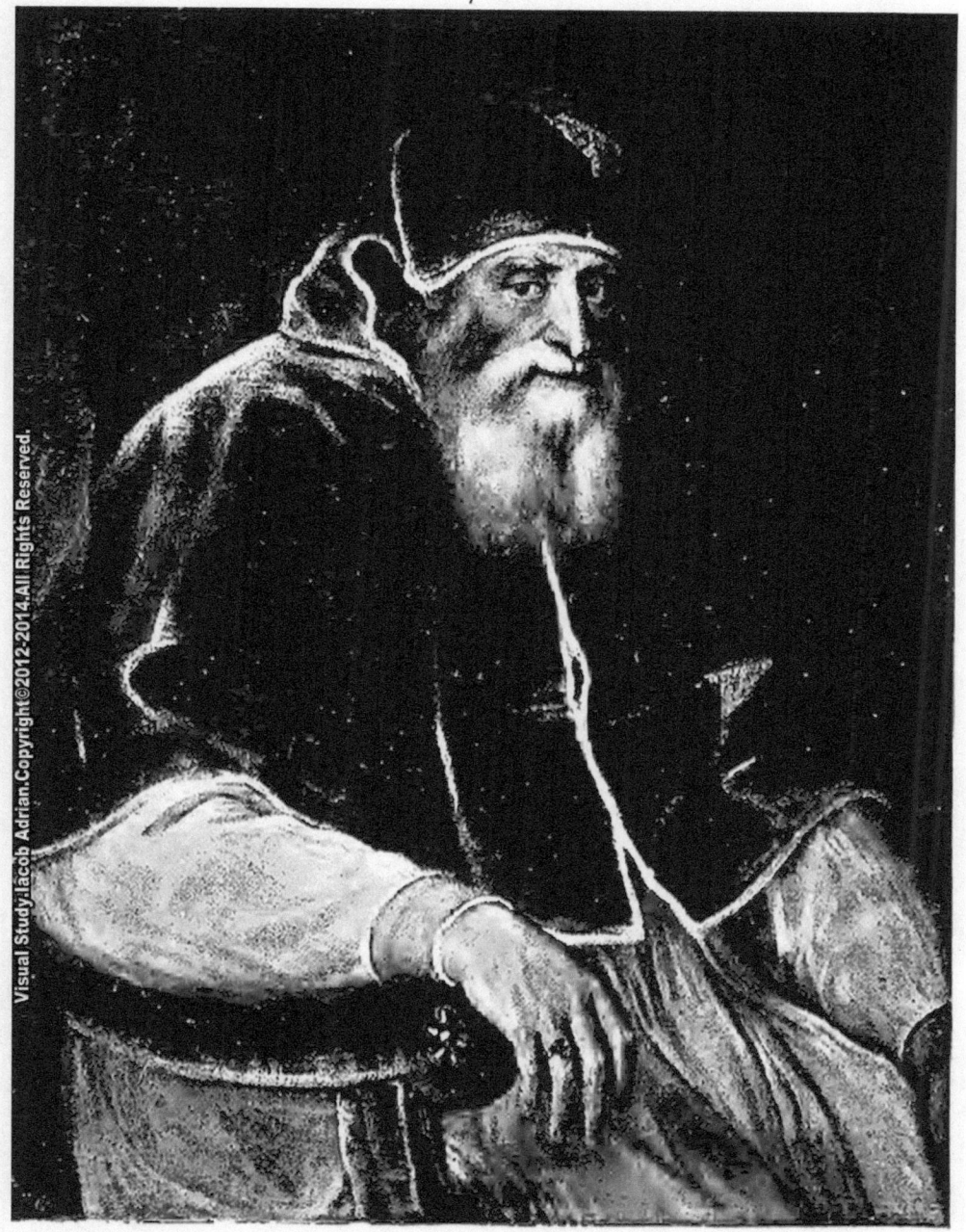

POPE PAUL III.   LE PAPE PAUL III.
(*The Hermitage, St. Petersburg*) (*L'Ermitage, Saint-Pétersbourg*)
PAPST PAUL III.
(*Petersburg, Eremitage*)
F. Hanfstaengl, Photo.

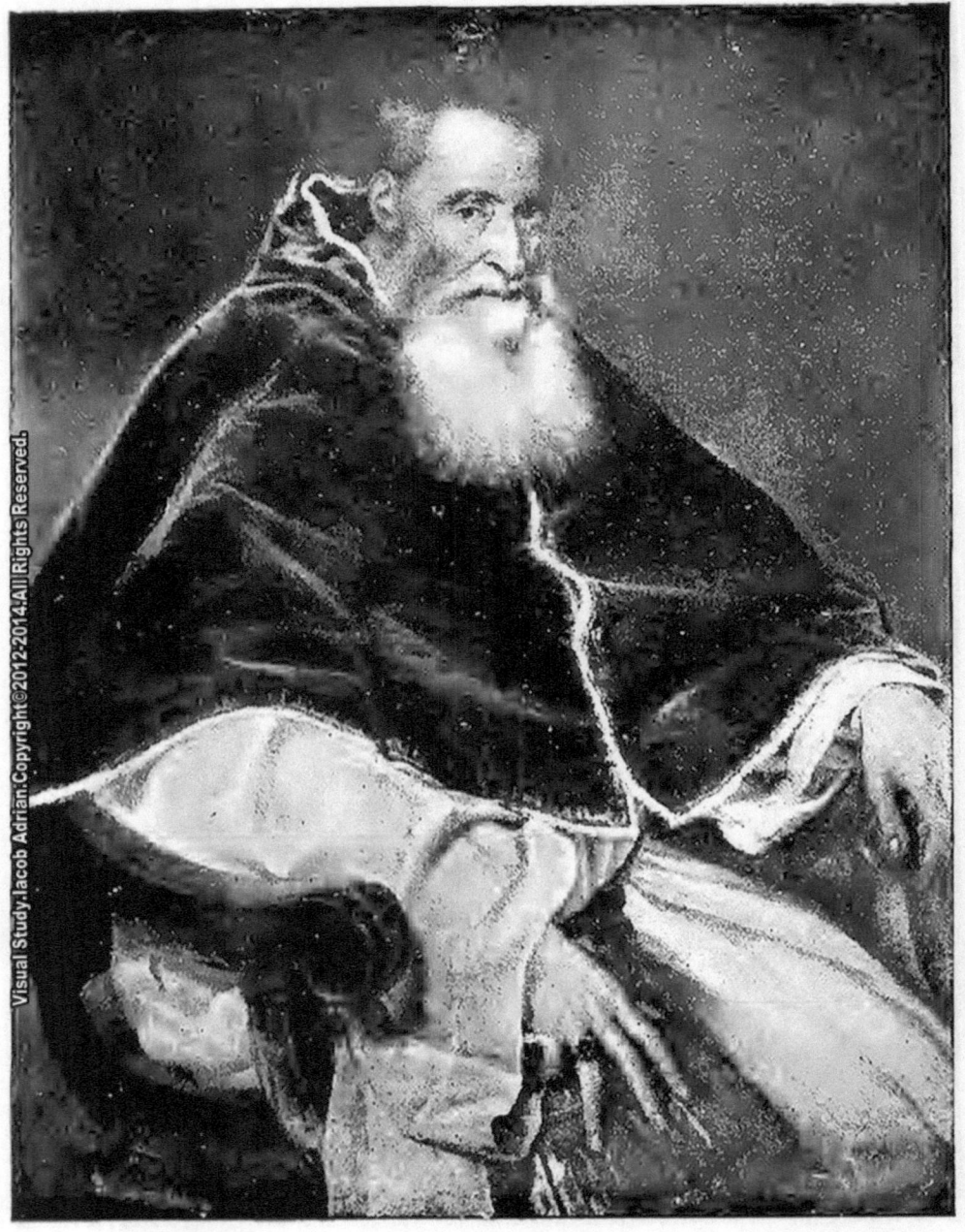

POPE PAUL III.
(*National Museum, Naples*)

LE PAPE PAUL III.
(*Musée national, Naples*)

PAPST PAUL III.
(*Neapel, Nationalmuseum*)

F. Hanfstaengl, Photo.

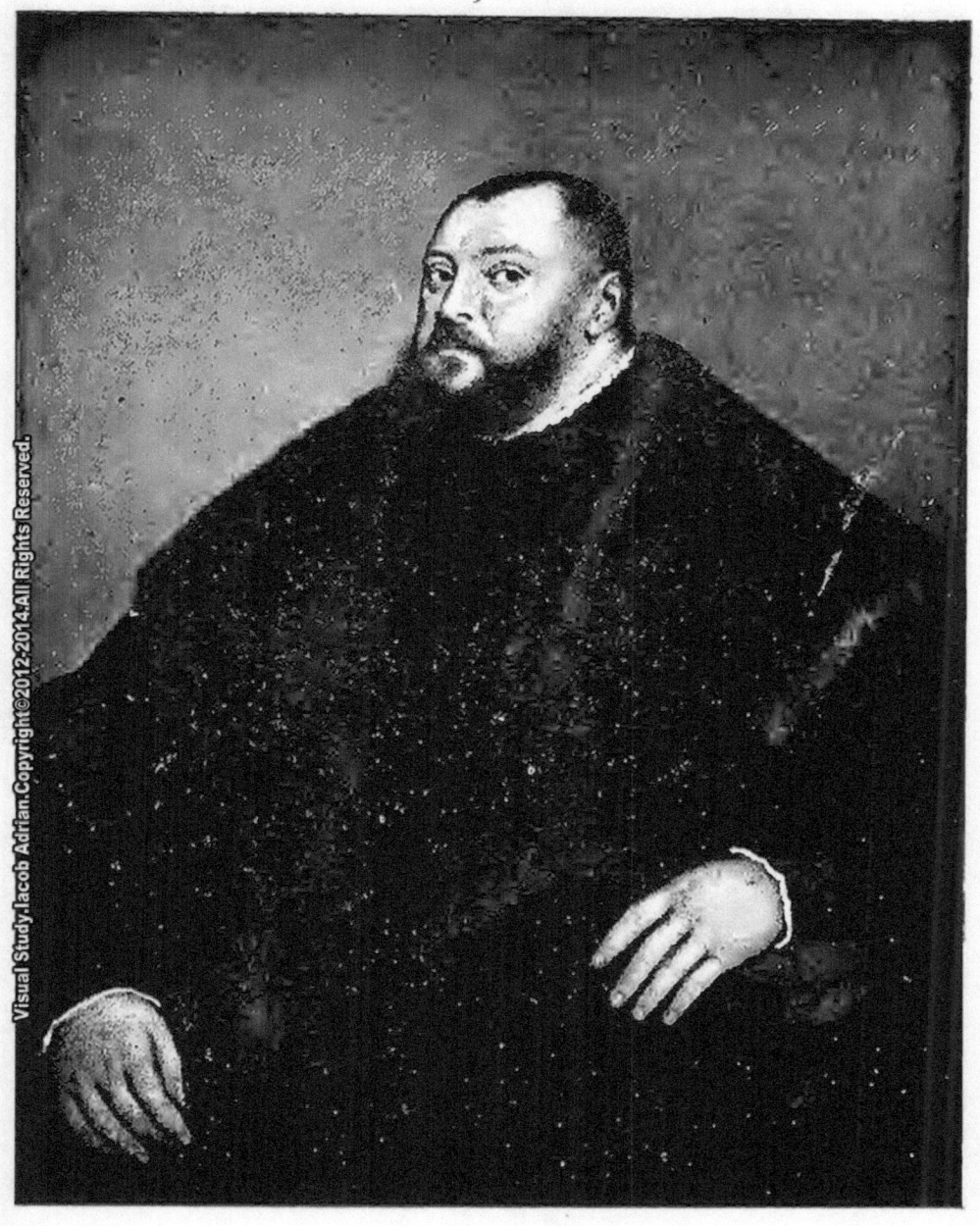

JOHN FREDERICK, ELECTOR OF   L'ÉLECTEUR JEAN-FRÉDÉRIC
SAXONY   DE SAXE
(*Imperial Gallery, Vienna*)   (*Galerie impériale, Vienne*)
KURFÜRST JOHANN FRIEDRICH VON SACHSEN
(*Wien, Kaiserl. Galerie*)
F. Hanfstaengl, Photo.

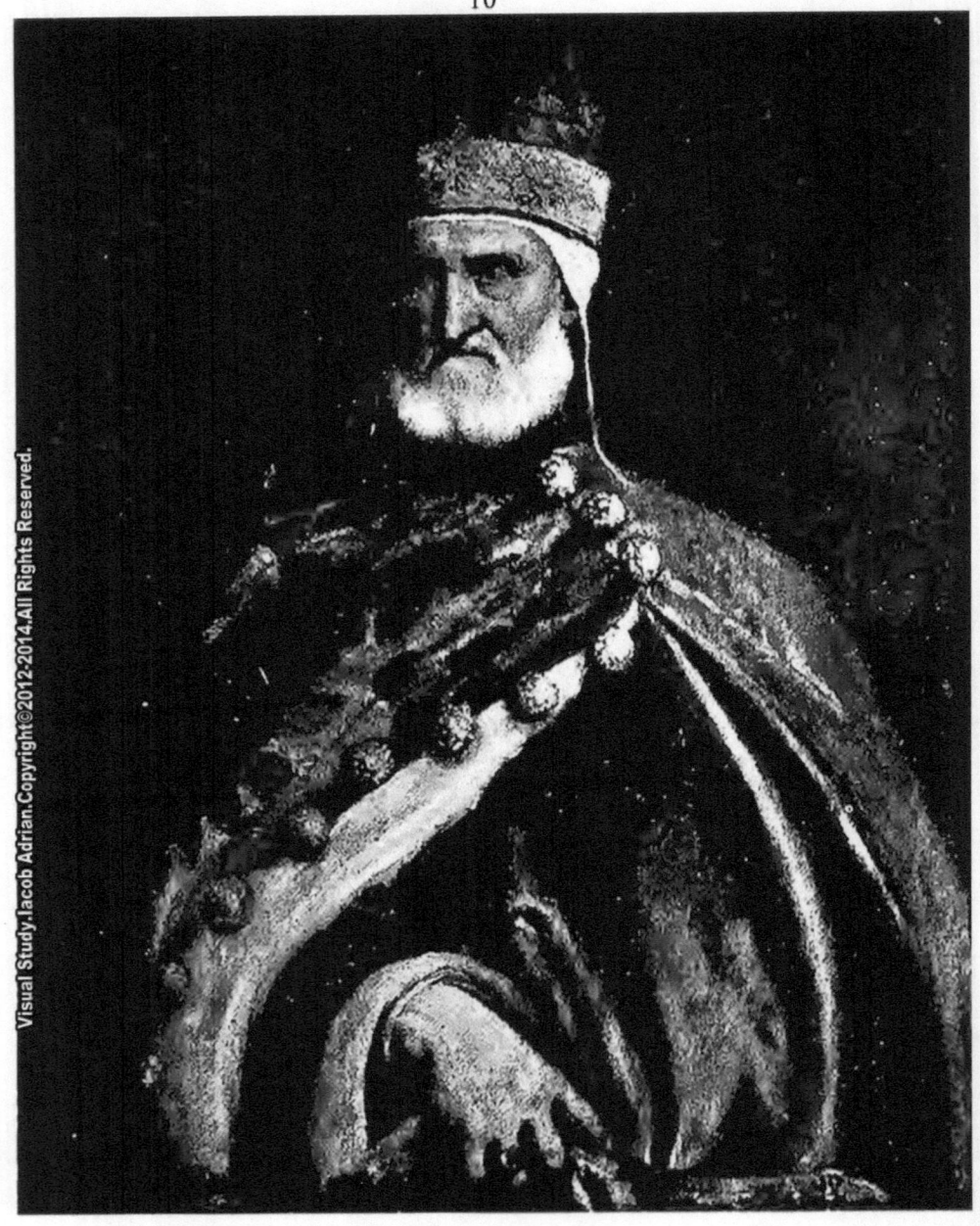

ANDREA GRITTI,
DOGE OF VENICE
(Czernin Gallery, Vienna)

ANDRÉ GRITTI,
DOGE DE VENISE
(Galerie Czernin, Vienne)

ANDREAS GRITTI, DOGE VON VENEDIG
(Wien, Czernin Galerie)
F. Hanfstaengl, Photo.

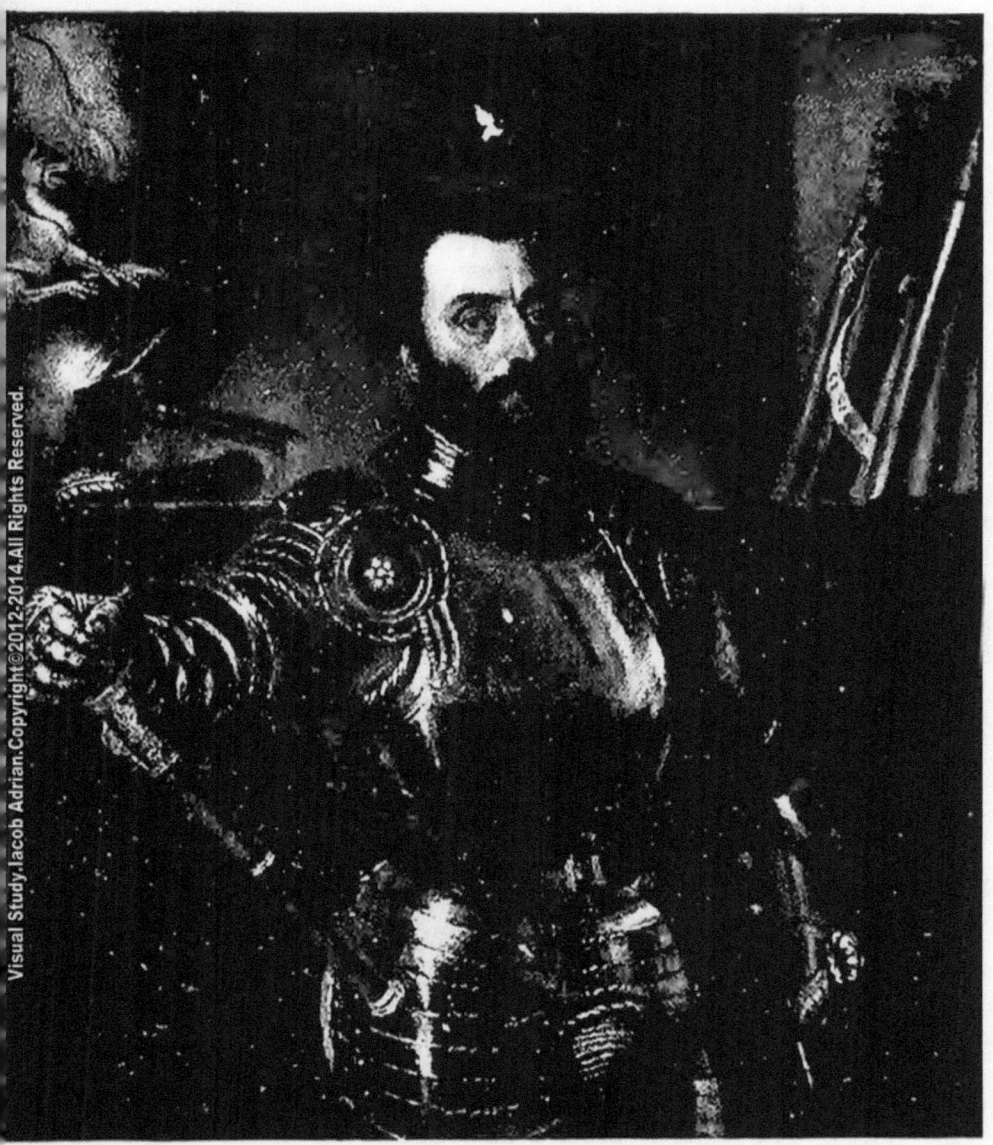

THE DUKE OF URBINO
(*Uffizi, Florence*)

LE DUC D'URBIN
(*Galerie des Uffizi, Florence*)

DER HERZOG VON URBINO
(*Florenz, Uffizien*)
F. Hanfstaengl, Photo.

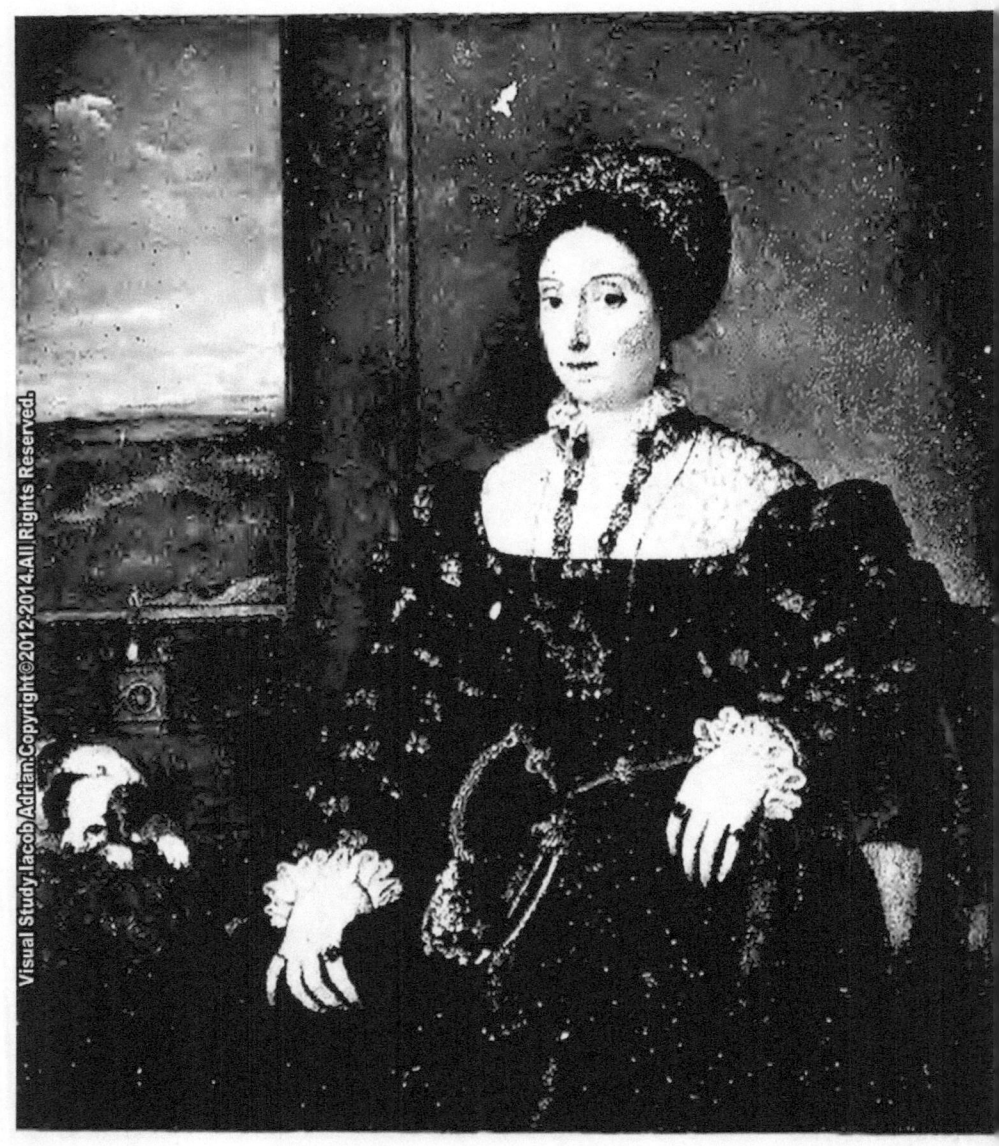

THE DUCHESS OF URBINO   LA DUCHESSE D'URBIN
(*Uffizi, Florence*)   (*Galerie des Uffizi, Florence*)
DIE HERZOGIN VON URBINO
(*Florenz, Uffizien*)
F. Hanfstaengl, Photo.

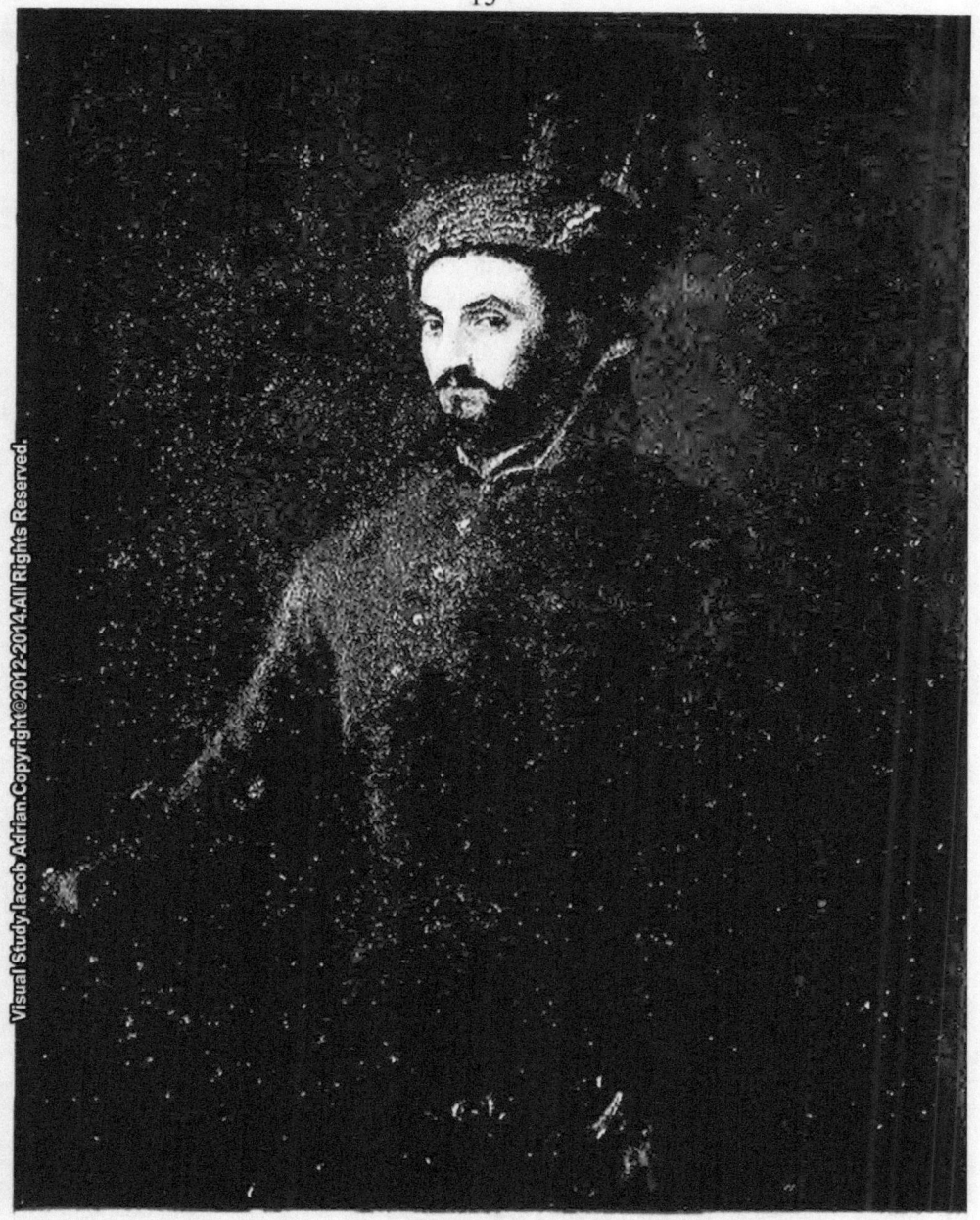

CARDINAL IPPOLITO DE'MEDICI
(*Pitti, Florence*)

LE CARDINAL HIPPOLYTE
DE MÉDICIS
(*Galerie Pitti, Florence*)

DER KARDINAL IPPOLITO DE'MEDICI
(*Florenz, Galerie Pitti*)
F. Hanfstaengl, Photo.

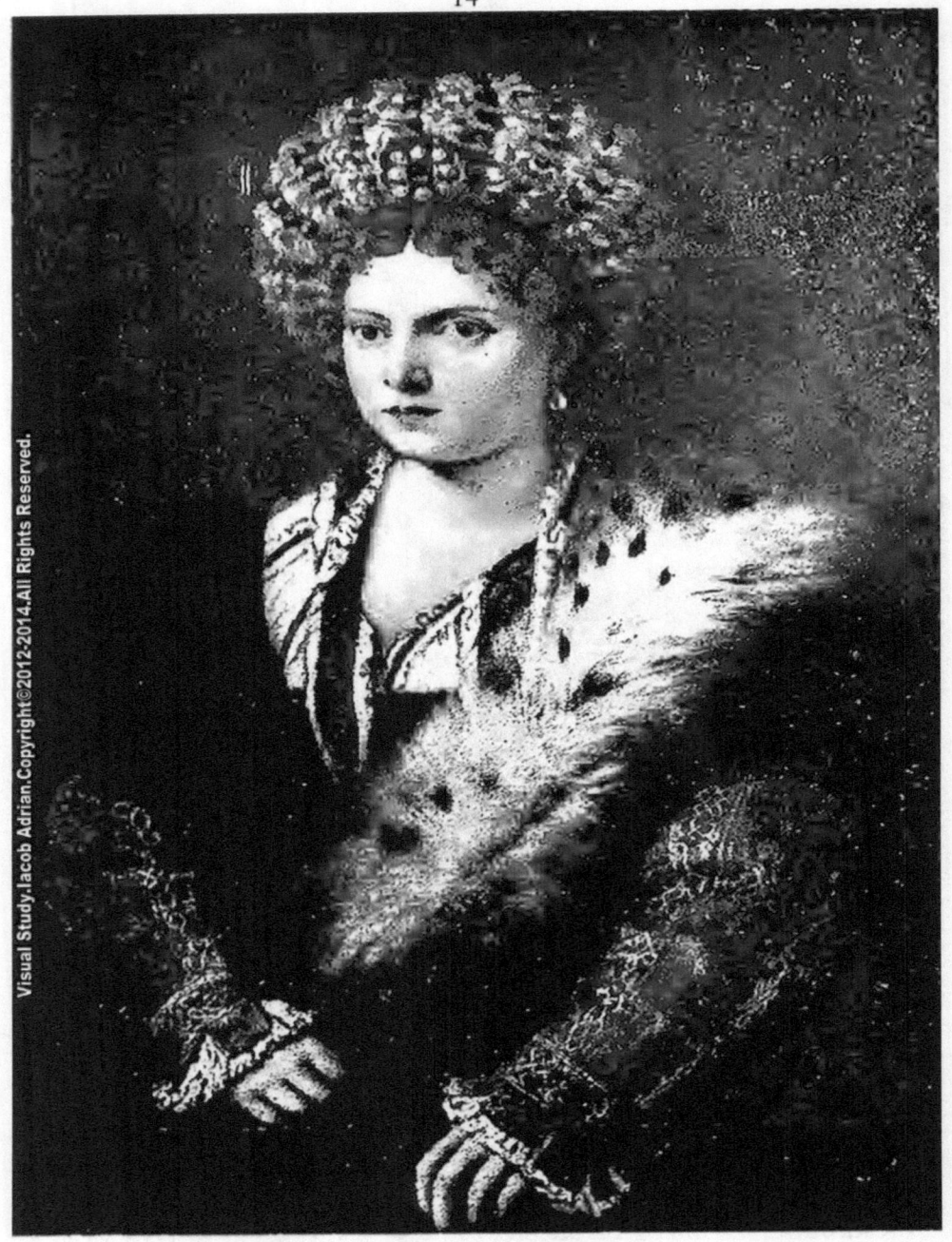

ISABELLA D'ESTE
(*Imperial Gallery, Vienna*)

ISABELLE D'ESTE
(*Galerie impériale, Vienne*)

ISABELLA D'ESTE
(*Wien, Kaiserl. Galerie*)
F. Hanfstaengl, Photo.

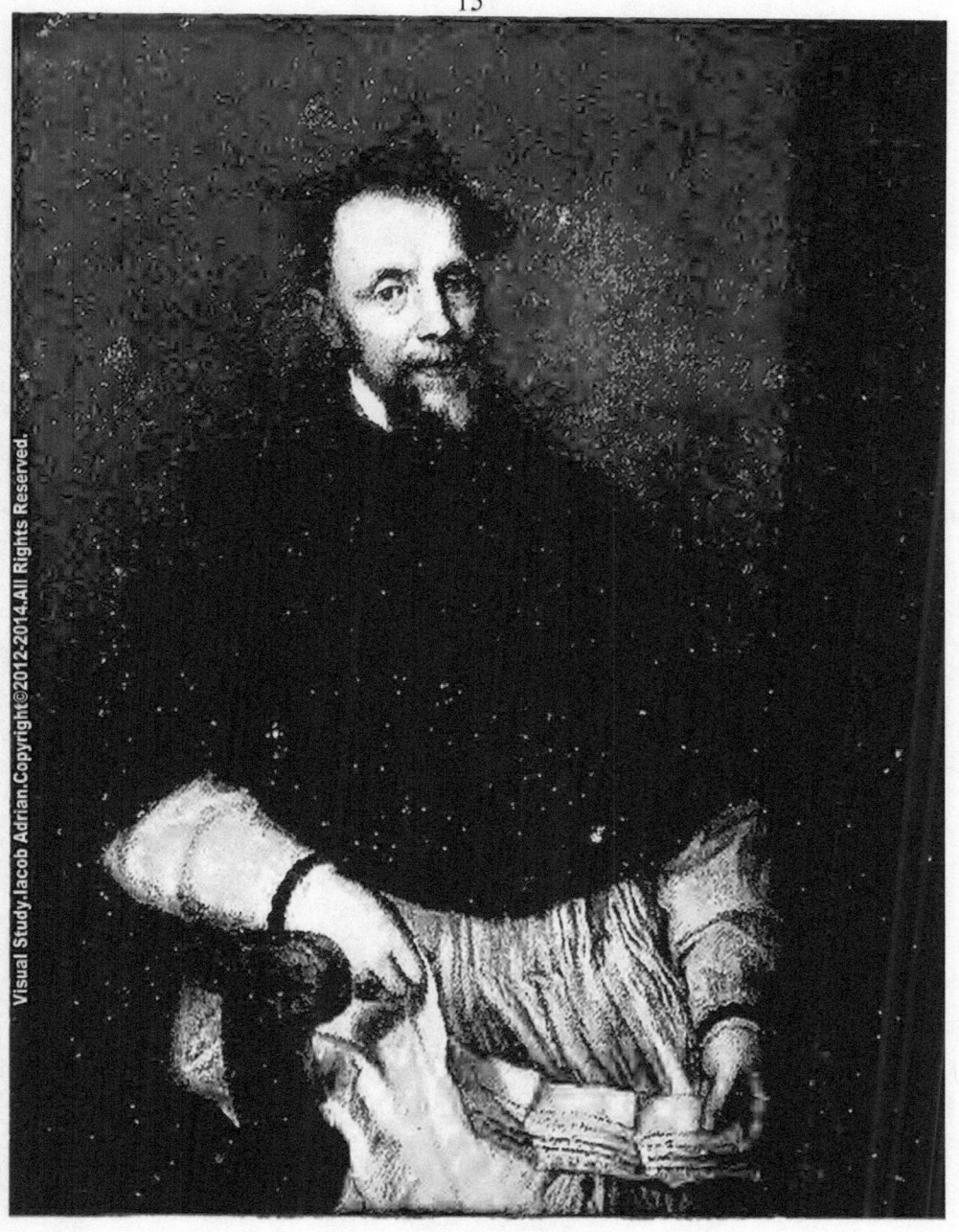

MONSIGNORE BECCADELLI   MONSEIGNEUR BECCADELLI
(*Uffizi, Florence*)   (*Galerie des Uffizi, Florence*)
ERZBISCHOF BECCADELLI
(*Florenz, Uffizien*)
F. Hanfstaengl, Photo.

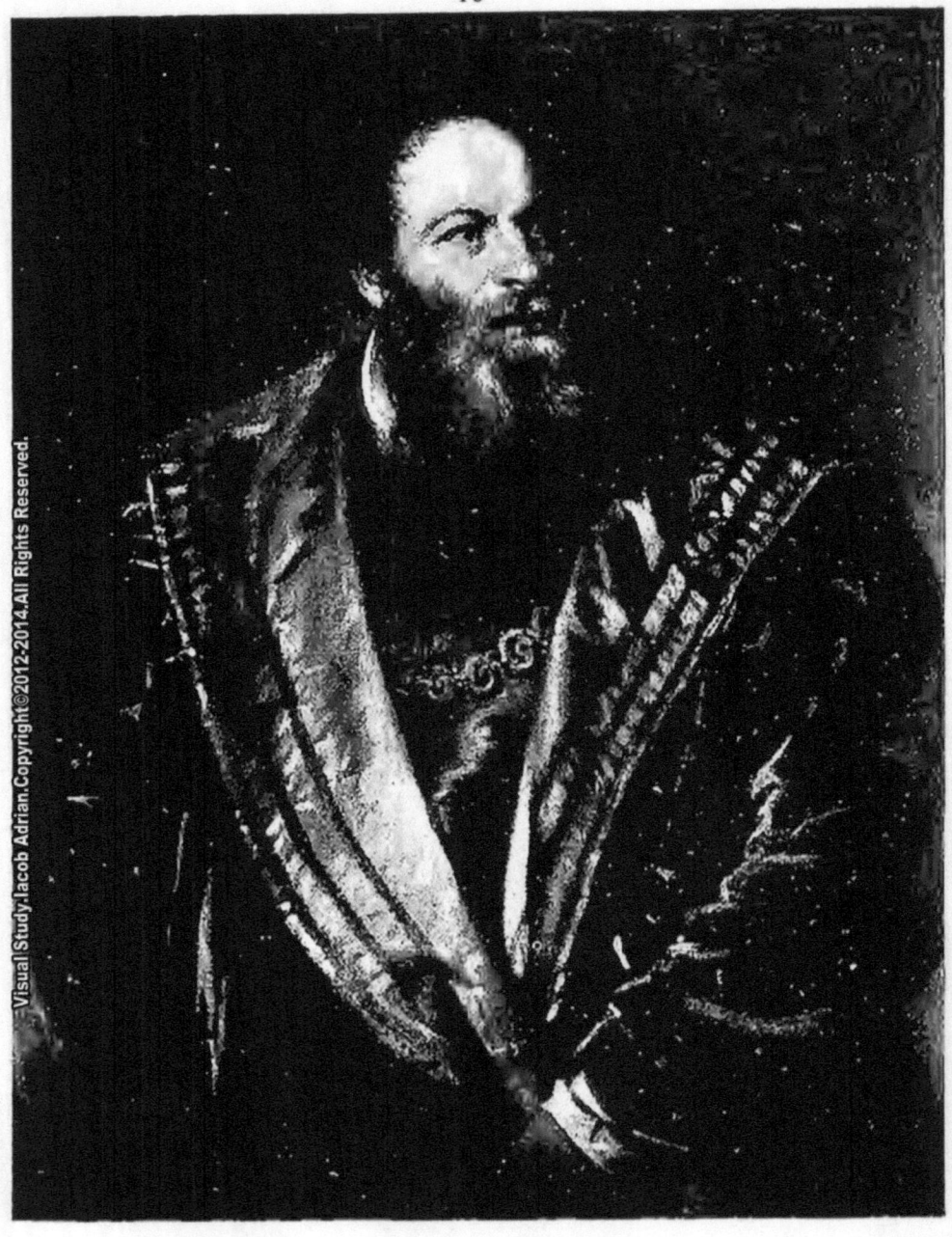

PIETRO ARETINO
(*Pitti, Florence*)

PIERRE ARÉTIN
(*Galerie Pitti, Florence*)

PIETRO ARETINO
(*Florenz, Galerie Pitti*)
F. Hanfstaengl, Photo.

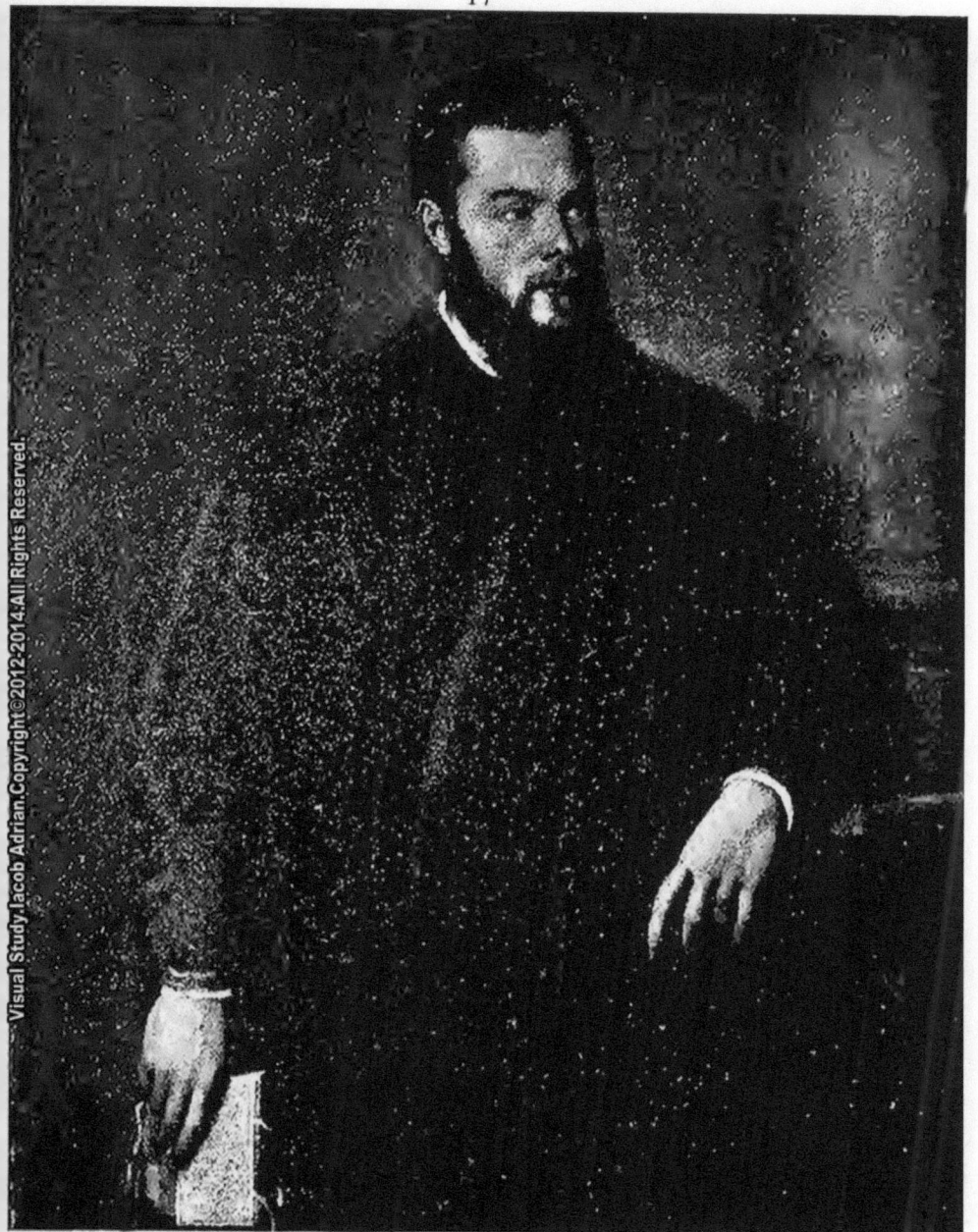

BENEDETTO VARCHI
(*Imperial Gallery, Vienna*)

BENEDETTO VARCHI
(*Galerie impériale, Vienne*)

BENEDETTO VARCHI
(*Wien. Kaiserl. Galerie*)

F. Hanfstaengl, Photo.

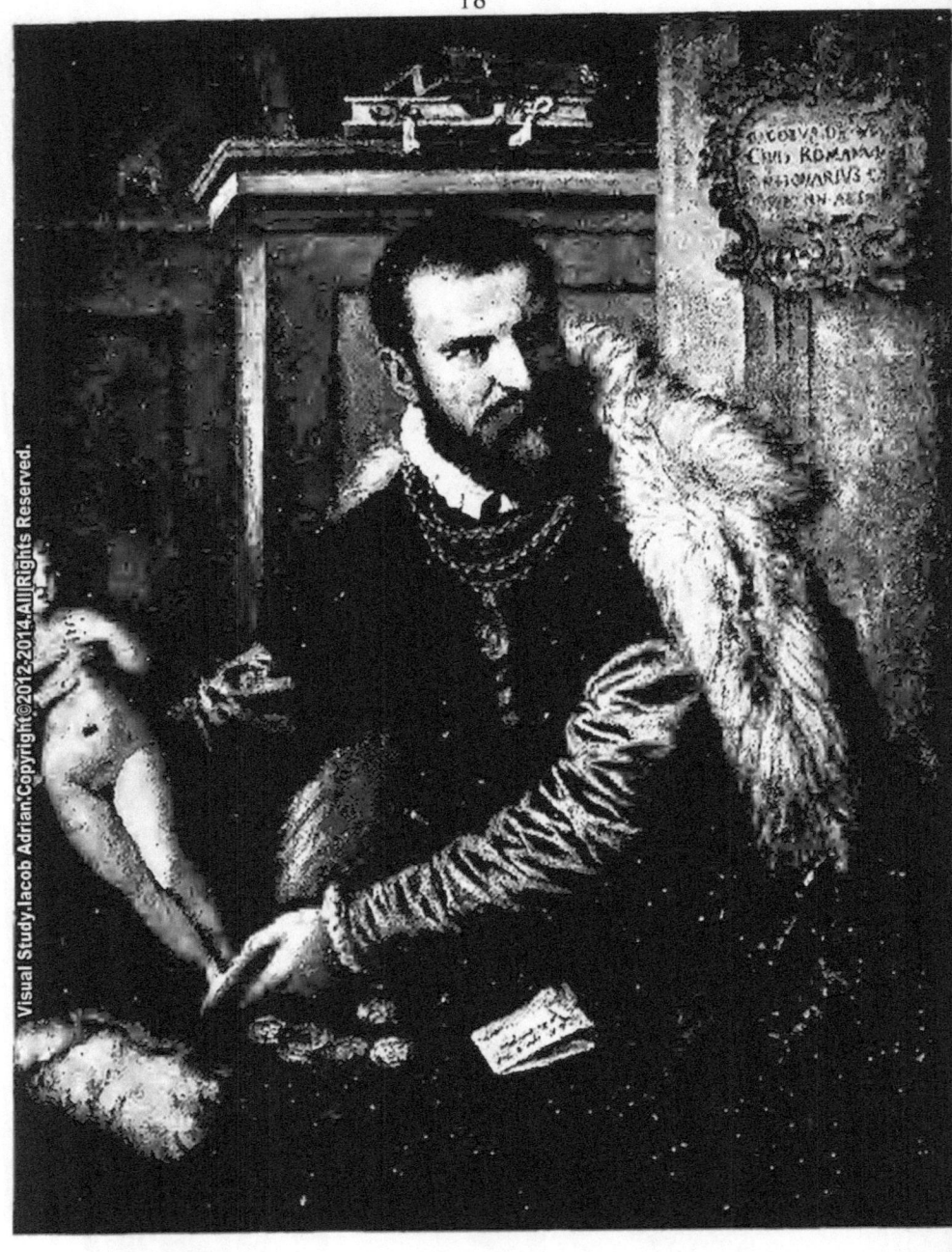

JACOPO DA STRADO
(*Imperial Gallery, Vienna*)

JACOPO DA STRADO
(*Galerie impériale, Vienne*)

JACOPO DA STRADO
(*Wien, Kaiserl. Galerie*)
F. Hanfstaengl, Photo.

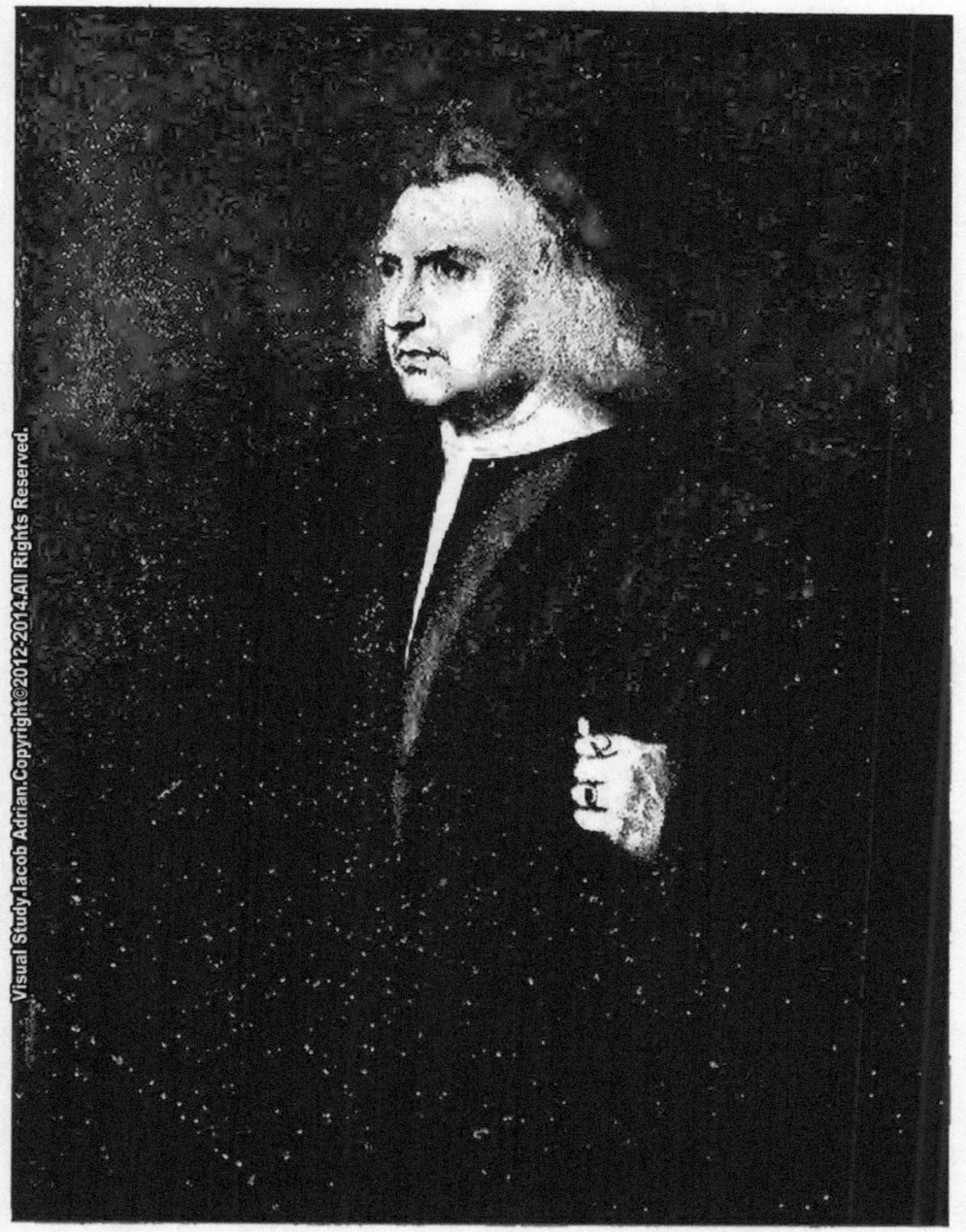

TITIAN'S PHYSICIAN, PARMA   PARMA, MÉDECIN DU TITIEN
(Imperial Gallery, Vienna)   *(Galerie impériale, Vienne)*
TIZIANS ARZT PARMA
(Wien, Kaiserl. Galerie)
F. Hanfstaengl, Photo.

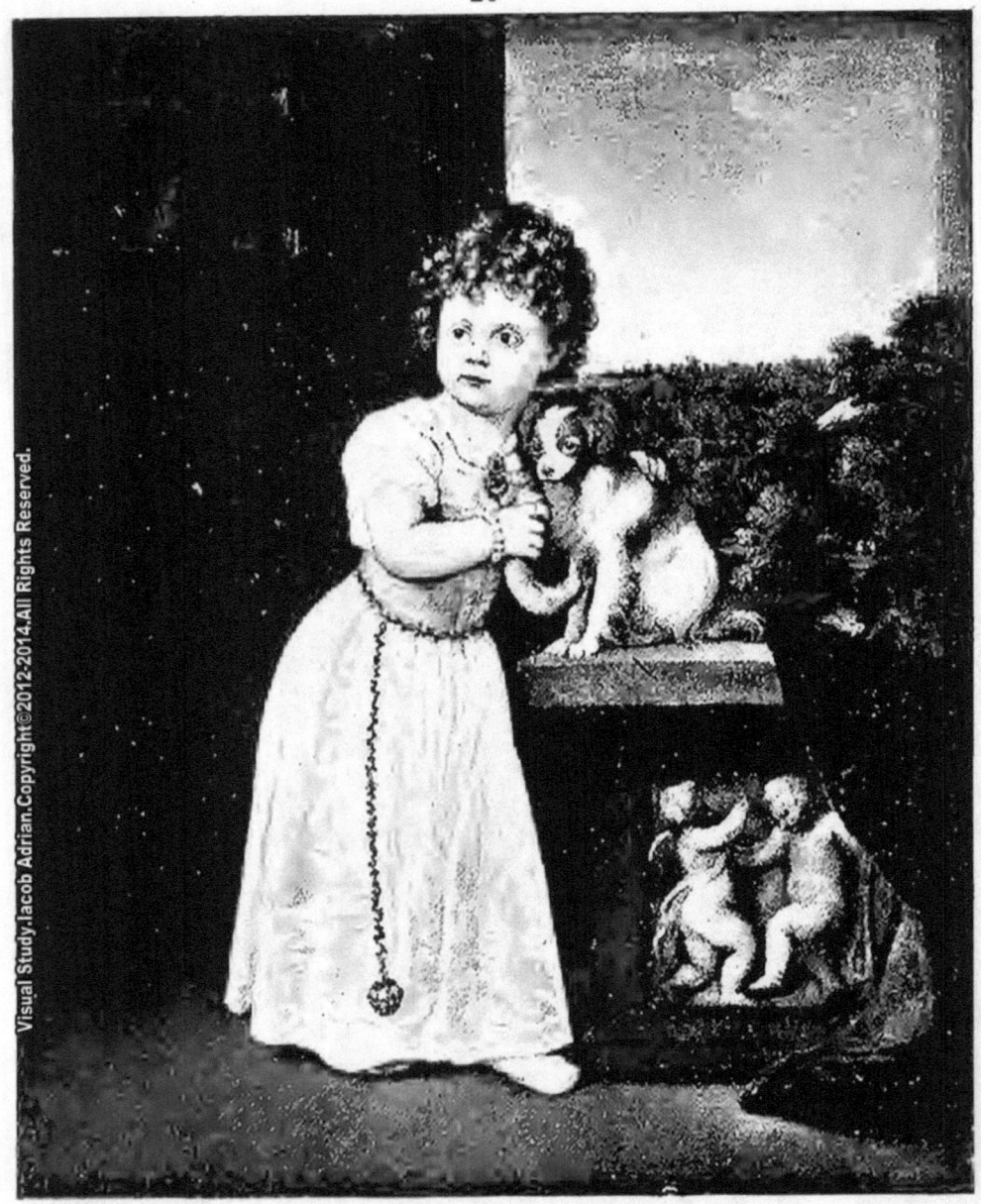

A DAUGHTER OF
ROBERTO STROZZI
(*Royal Gallery, Berlin*)

UNE FILLE DE
ROBERTO STROZZI
(*Musée royal, Berlin*)

EINE TOCHTER DES ROBERTO STROZZI
(*Berlin, Kgl. Galerie*)
F. Hanfstaengl, Photo.

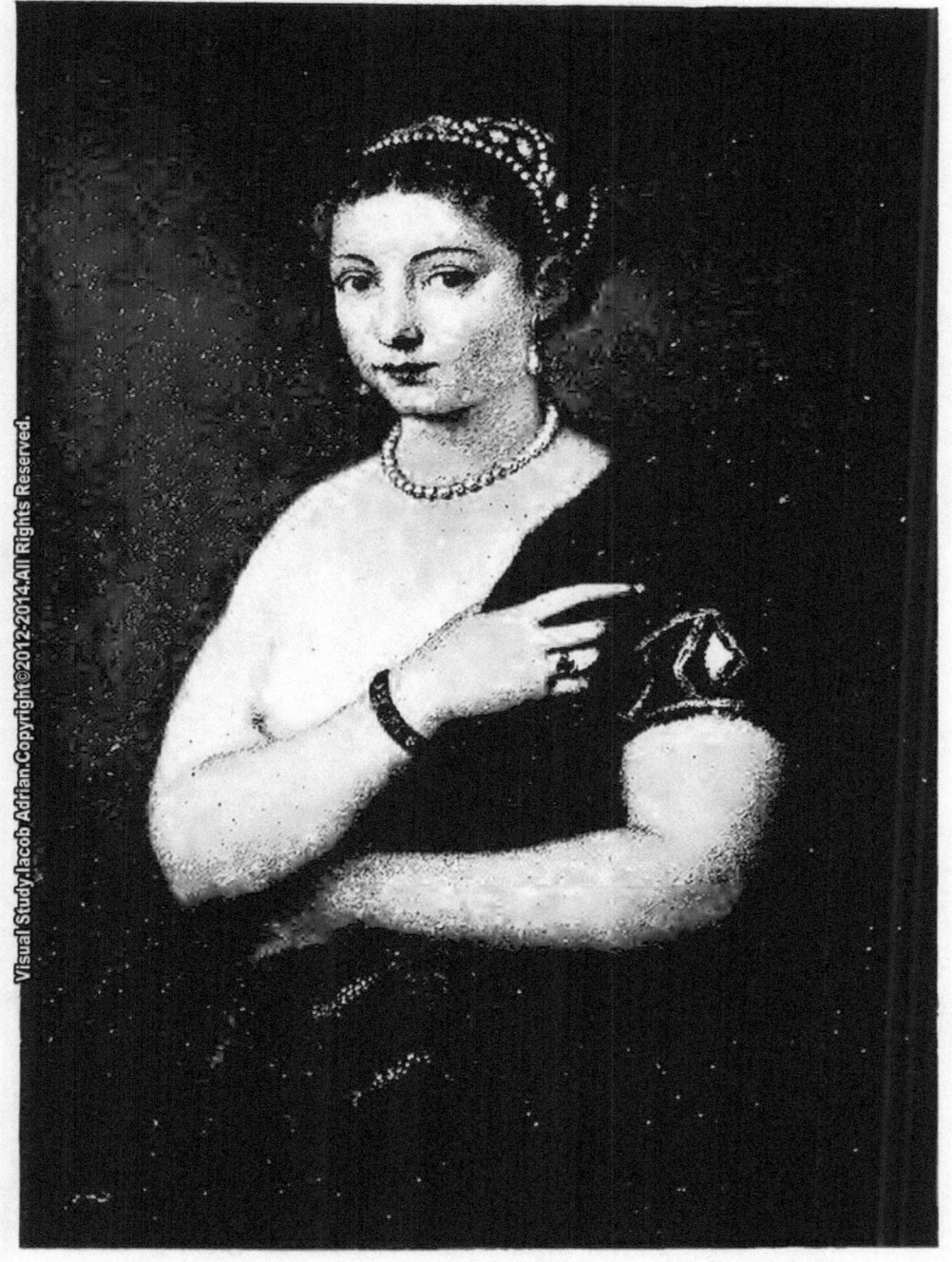

GIRL IN A FUR CLOAK
(*Imperial Gallery, Vienna*)

JEUNE FEMME AUX FOURRURES
(*Galerie impériale, Vienne*)

MÄDCHEN IM PELZ
(*Wien, Kaiserl. Galerie*)

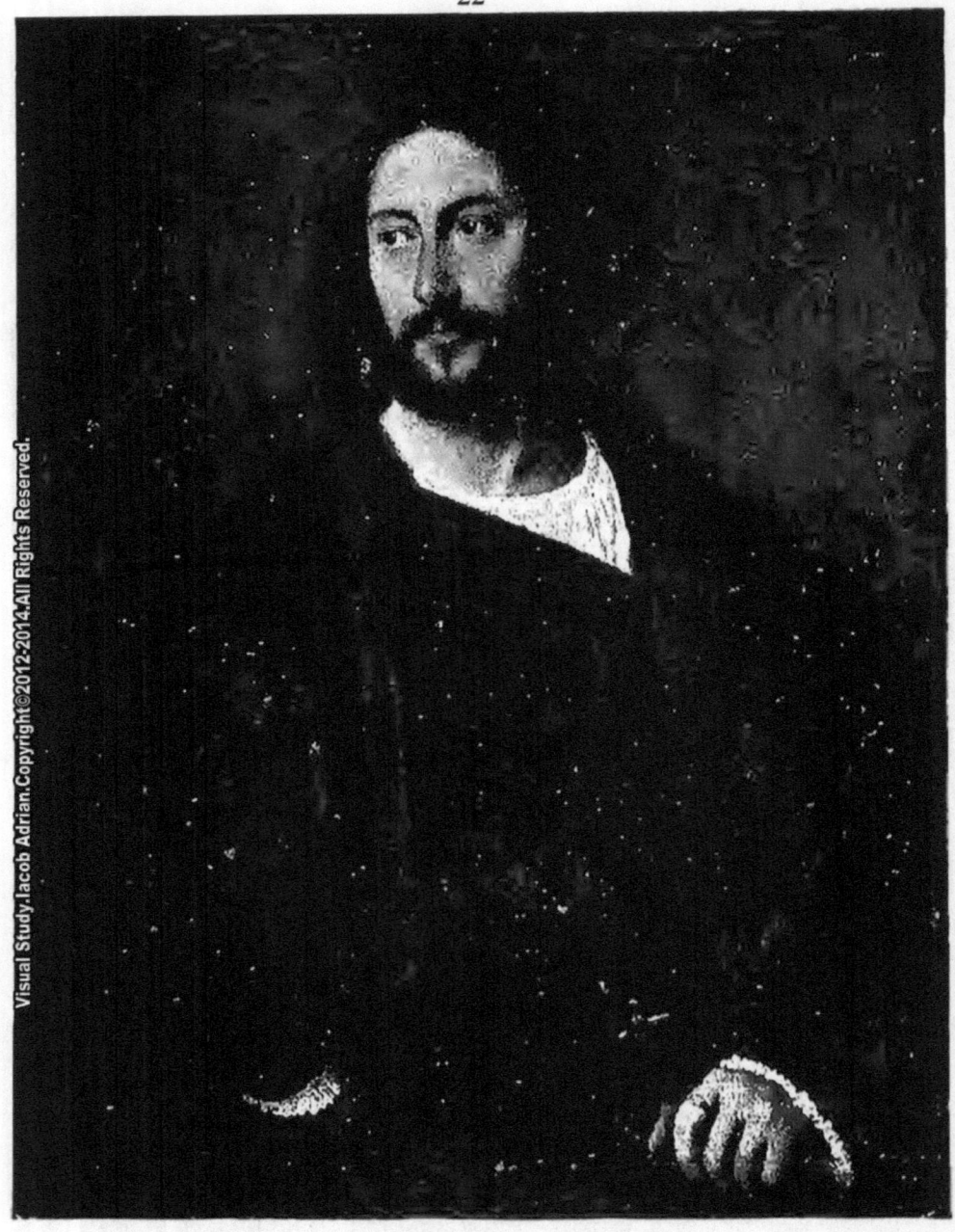

PORTRAIT OF A YOUNG MAN   PORTRAIT D'UN JEUNE HOMME
(*Pinakothek, Munich*)   (*Pinacothèque, Munich*)
BILDNIS EINES JUNGEN MANNES
(*München, Pinakothek*)
F. Hanfstaengl, Photo.

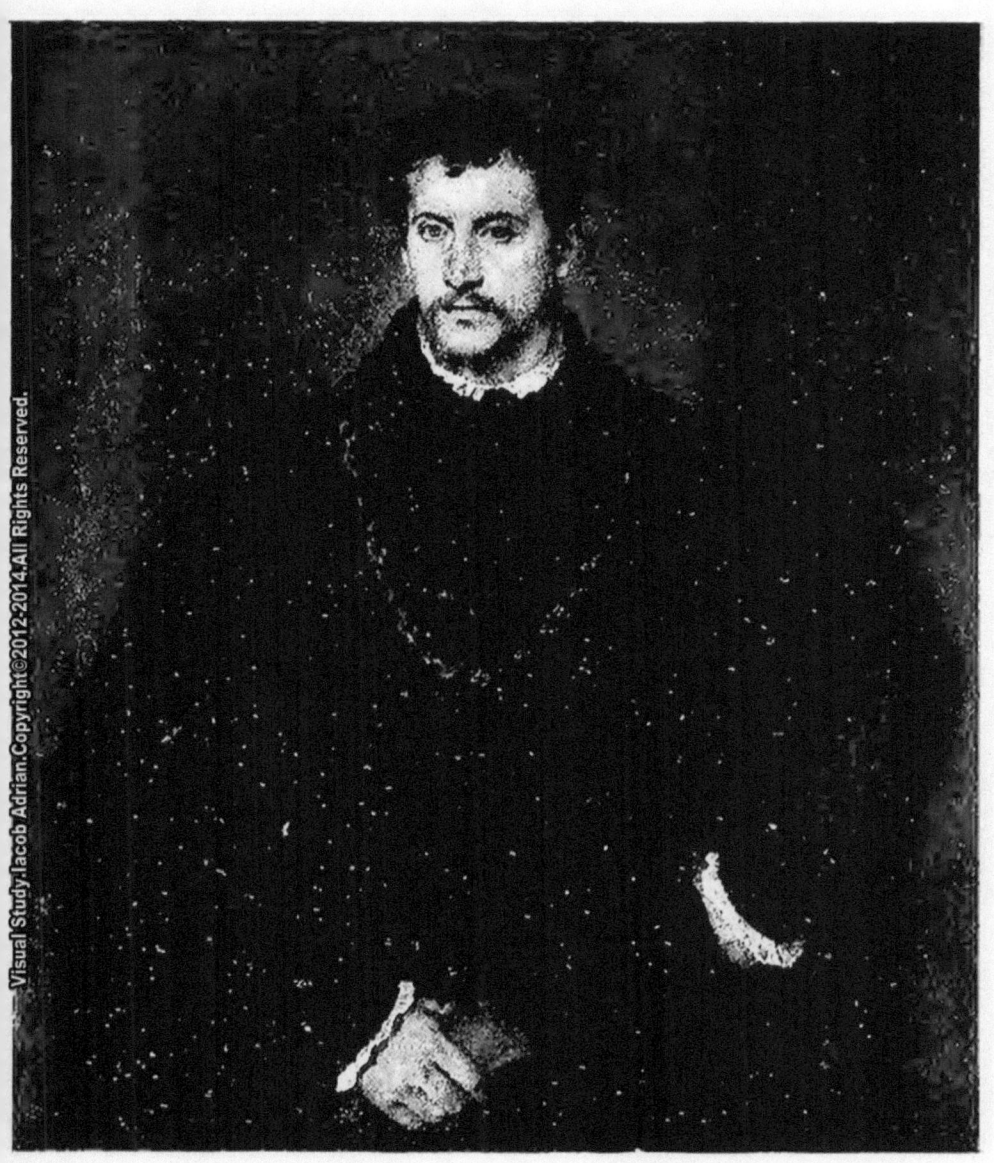

PORTRAIT OF A MAN   PORTRAIT D'HOMME
(*Pitti, Florence*)   (*Galerie Pitti, Florence*)

MÄNNLICHES BILDNIS
(*Florenz, Galerie Pitti*)
F. Hanfstaengl, Photo.

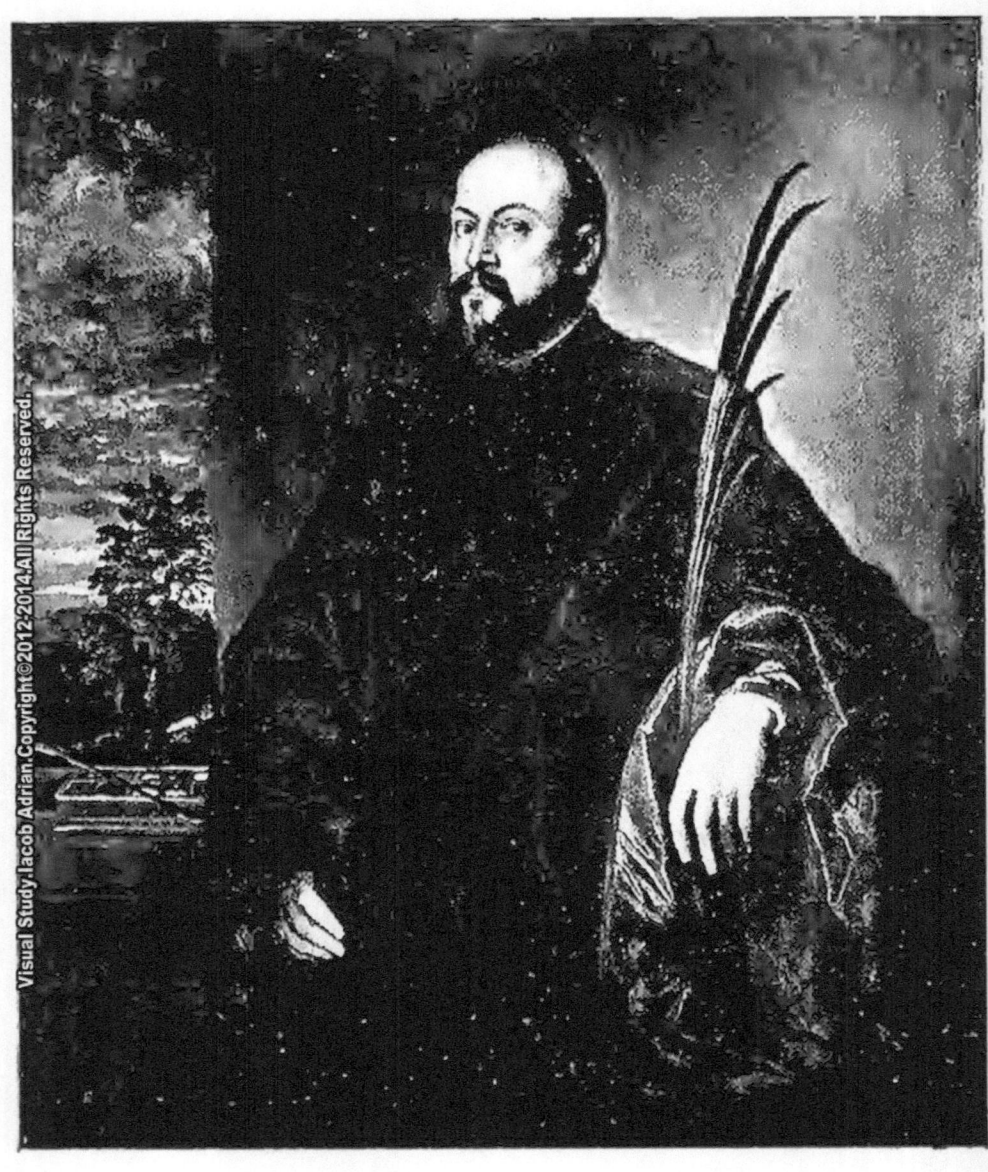

PORTRAIT OF A MAN   PORTRAIT D'HOMME
(*Royal Gallery, Dresden*)   (*Galerie royale, Dresde*)
MÄNNLICHES BILDNIS
(*Dresden, Kgl. Galerie*)
F. Hanfstaengl, Photo.

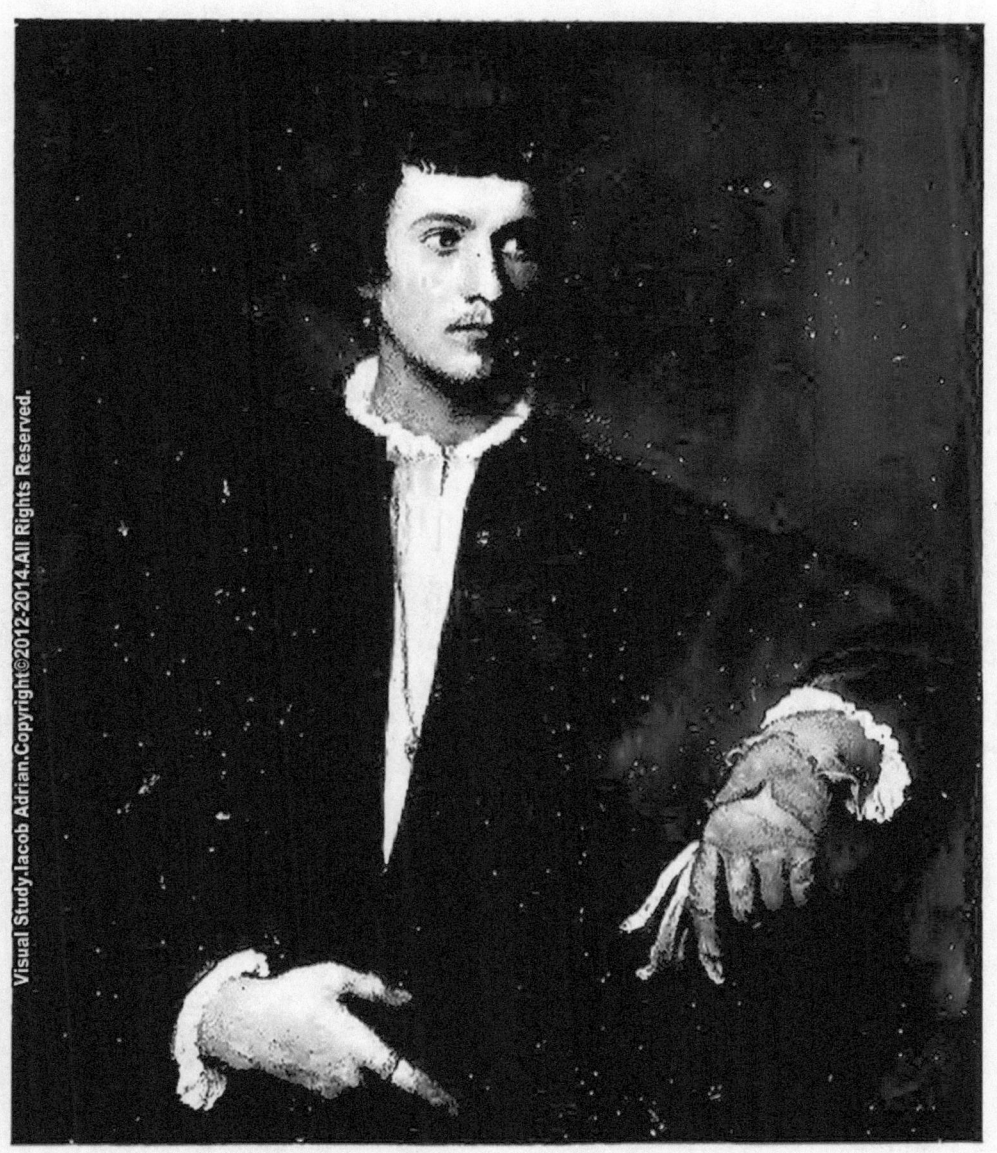

"L'Homme au Gant"
(*Louvre, Paris*)

L'Homme au Gant
(*Louvre, Paris*)

Der Mann mit dem Handschuh
(*Paris, Louvre*)

Braun, Clément & Co., Photo.

26

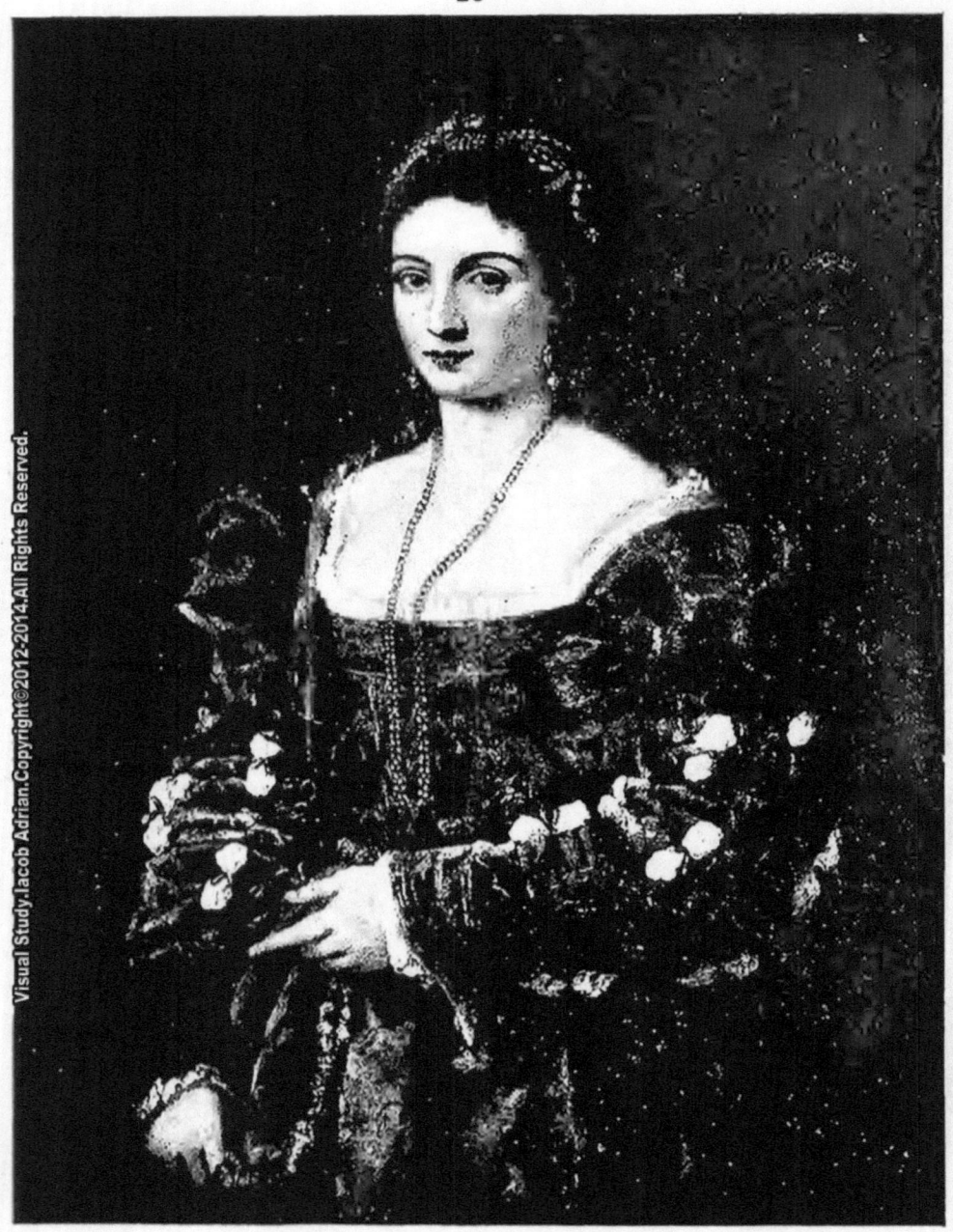

"LA BELLA"
(*Pitti, Florence*)

"LA BELLA"
(*Galerie Pitti, Florence*)

"LA BELLA"
(*Florenz, Galerie Pitti*)
F. Hanfstaengl, Photo.

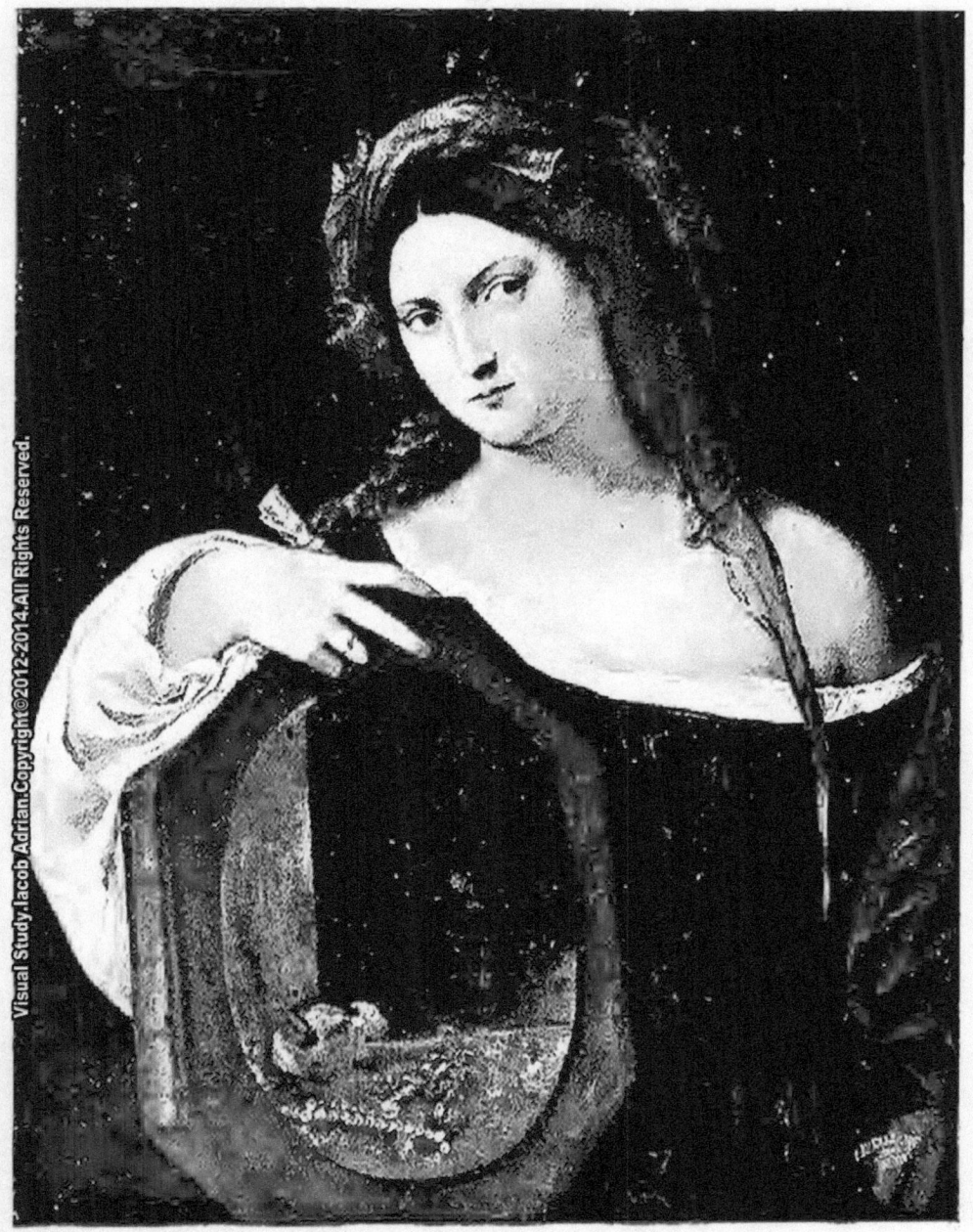

VANITY

(*Pinakothek, Munich*)

LA VANITÉ

(*Pinacothèque, Munich*)

DIE EITELKEIT

(*München, Pinakothek*)

F. Hanfstaengl, Photo.

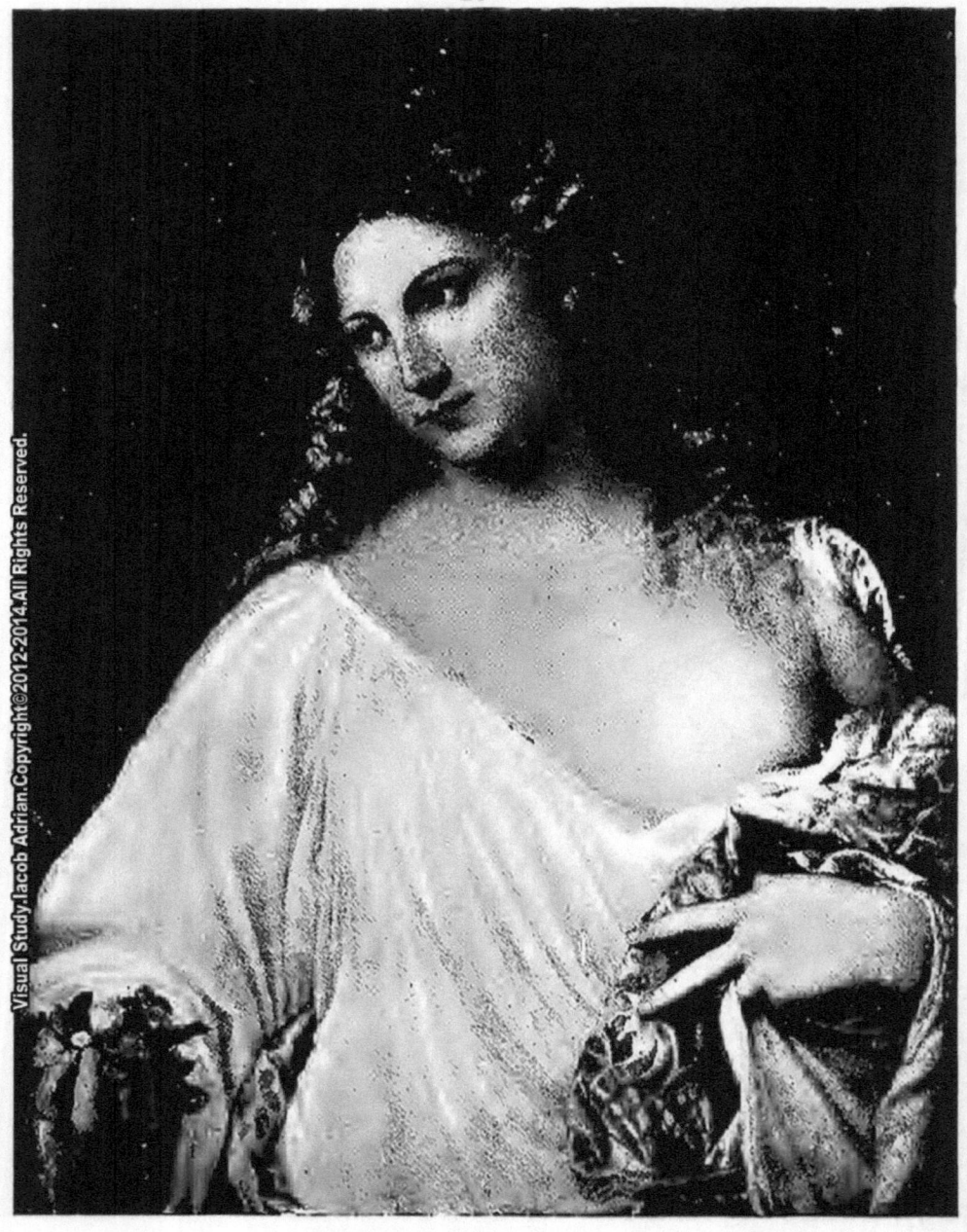

FLORA
(*Uffizi, Florence*)

LA FLORA
(*Galerie des Uffizi, Florence*)

LA FLORA
(*Florenz, Galerie Pitti*)
F. Hanfstaengl, Photo.

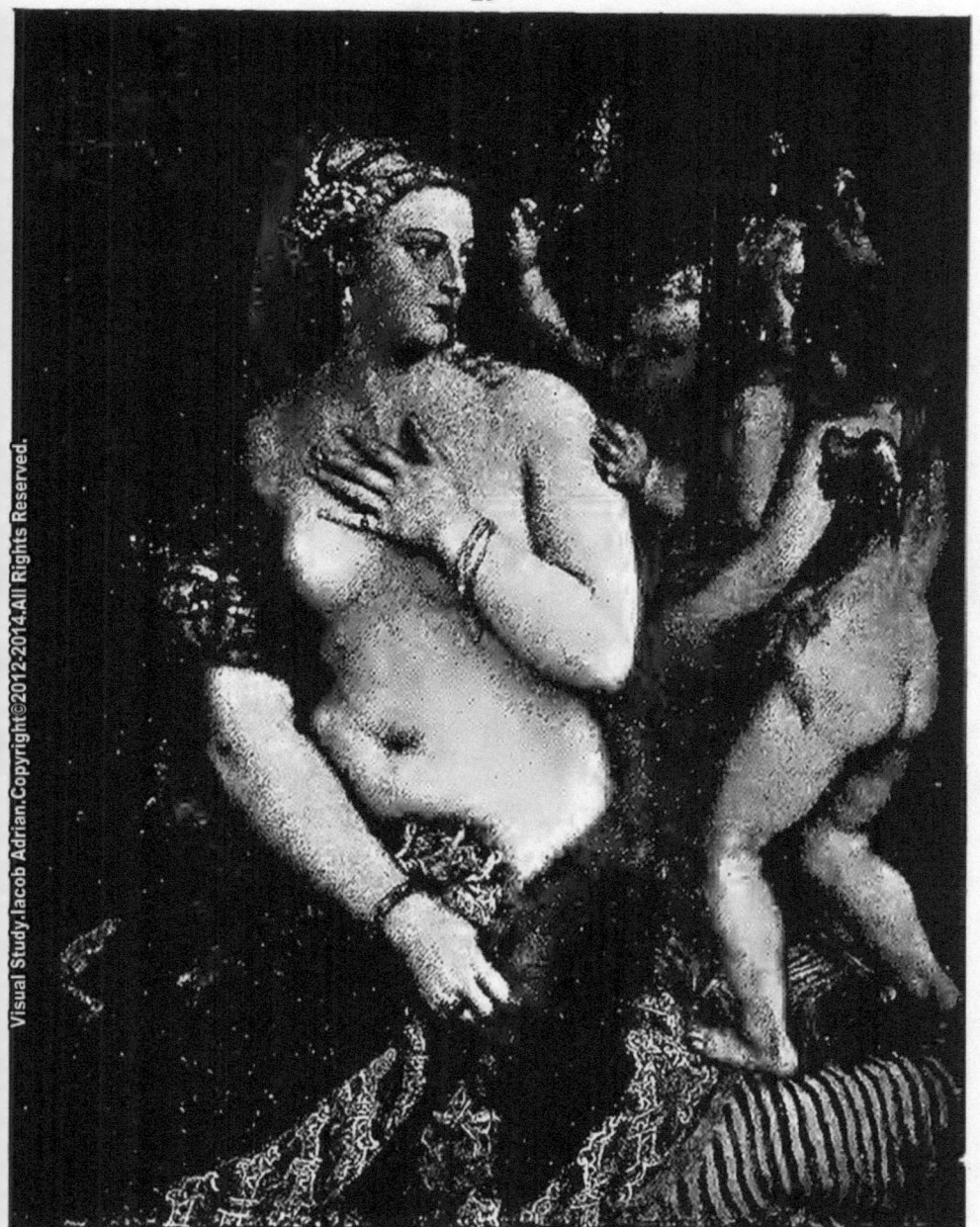

THE TOILET OF VENUS   LA TOILETTE DE VÉNUS
(*The Hermitage, St. Petersburg*) (*L'Ermitage, Saint-Pétersbourg*)
DIE TOILETTE DER VENUS
(*Petersburg, Eremitage*)
F. Hanfstaengl, Photo.

30

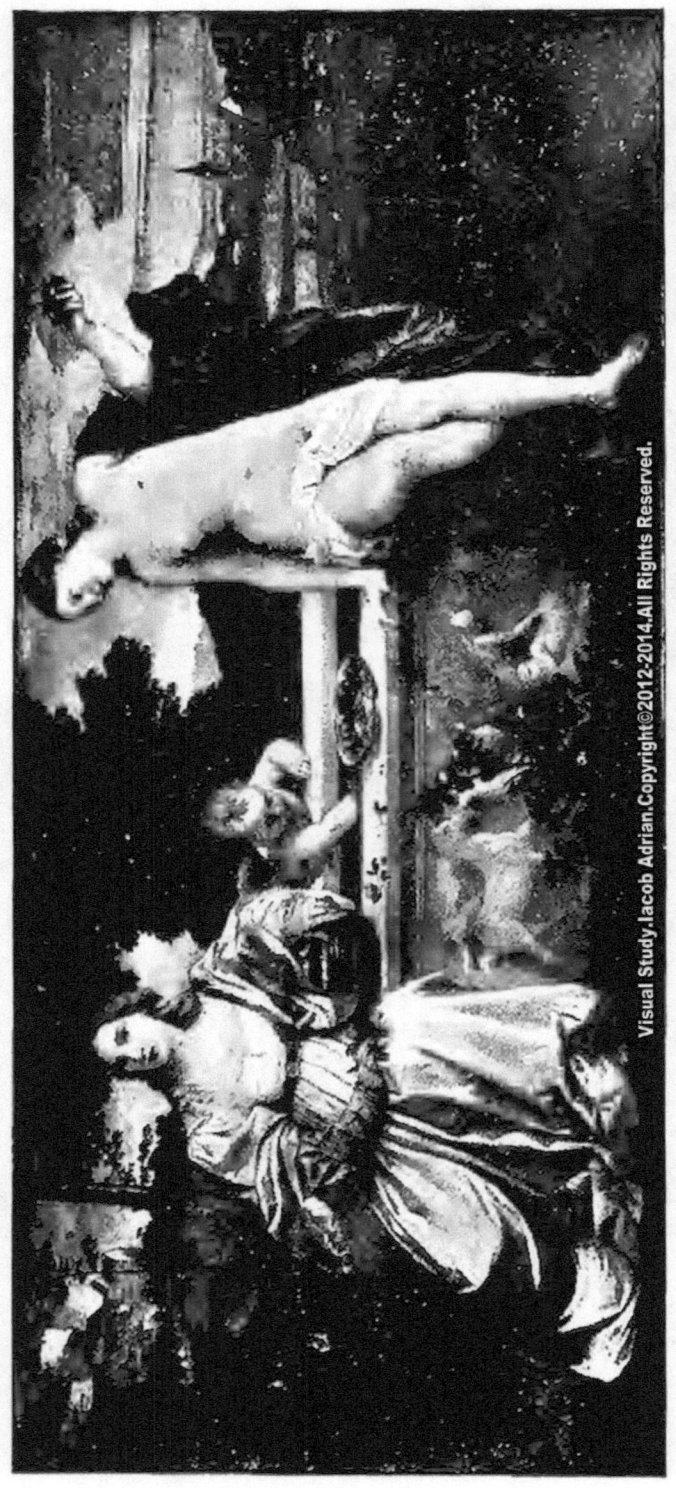

SACRED AND PROFANE LOVE   HIMMLISCHE UND IRDISCHE LIEBE   L'AMOUR SACRÉ ET L'AMOUR PROFANE
(*Borghese Gallery, Rome*)   (*Rom, Galerie Borghese*)   (*Galerie Borghèse, Rome*)

F. Hanfstaengl, Photo.

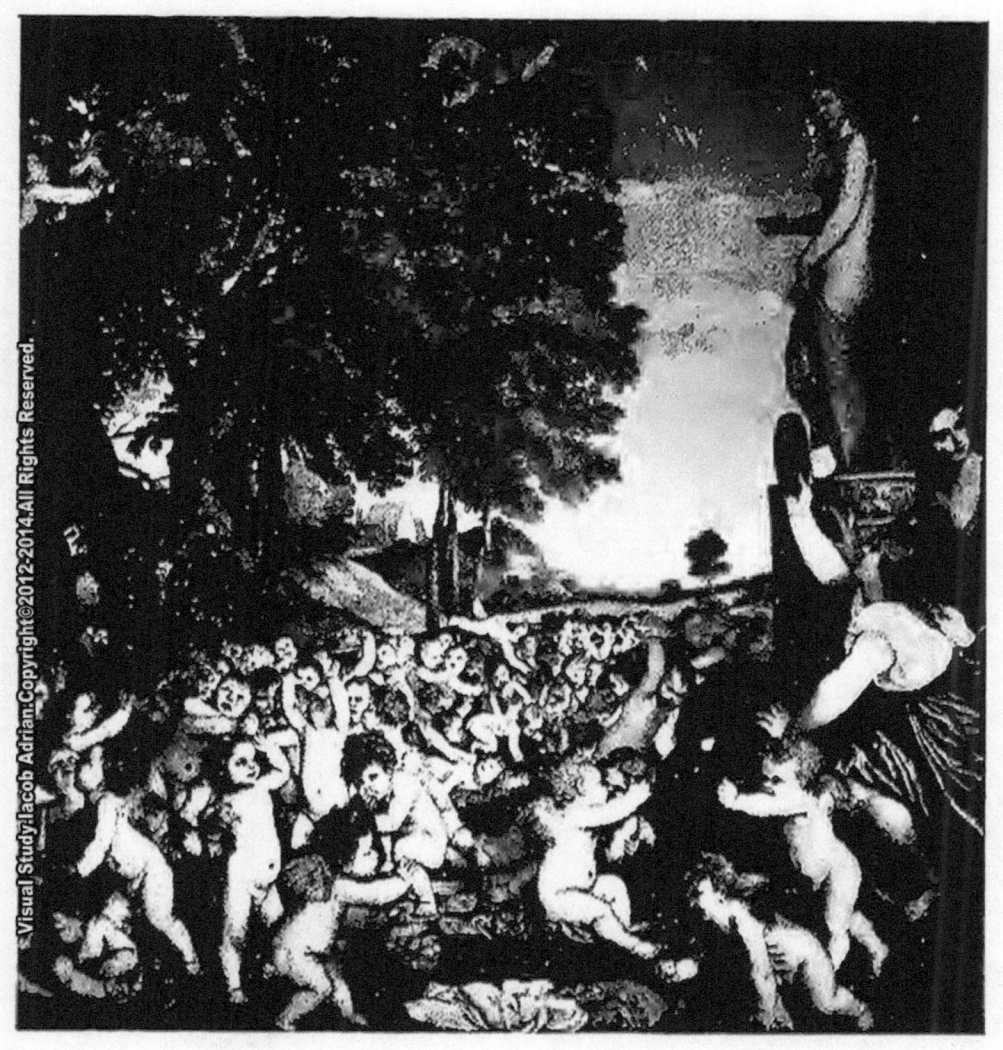

THE WORSHIP OF VENUS   OFFRANDE À LA DÉESSE DES AMOURS
(Prado, Madrid)   *(Prado, Madrid)*
DAS VENUSFEST
(Madrid, Prado)
Braun, Clément & Co., Photo.

32

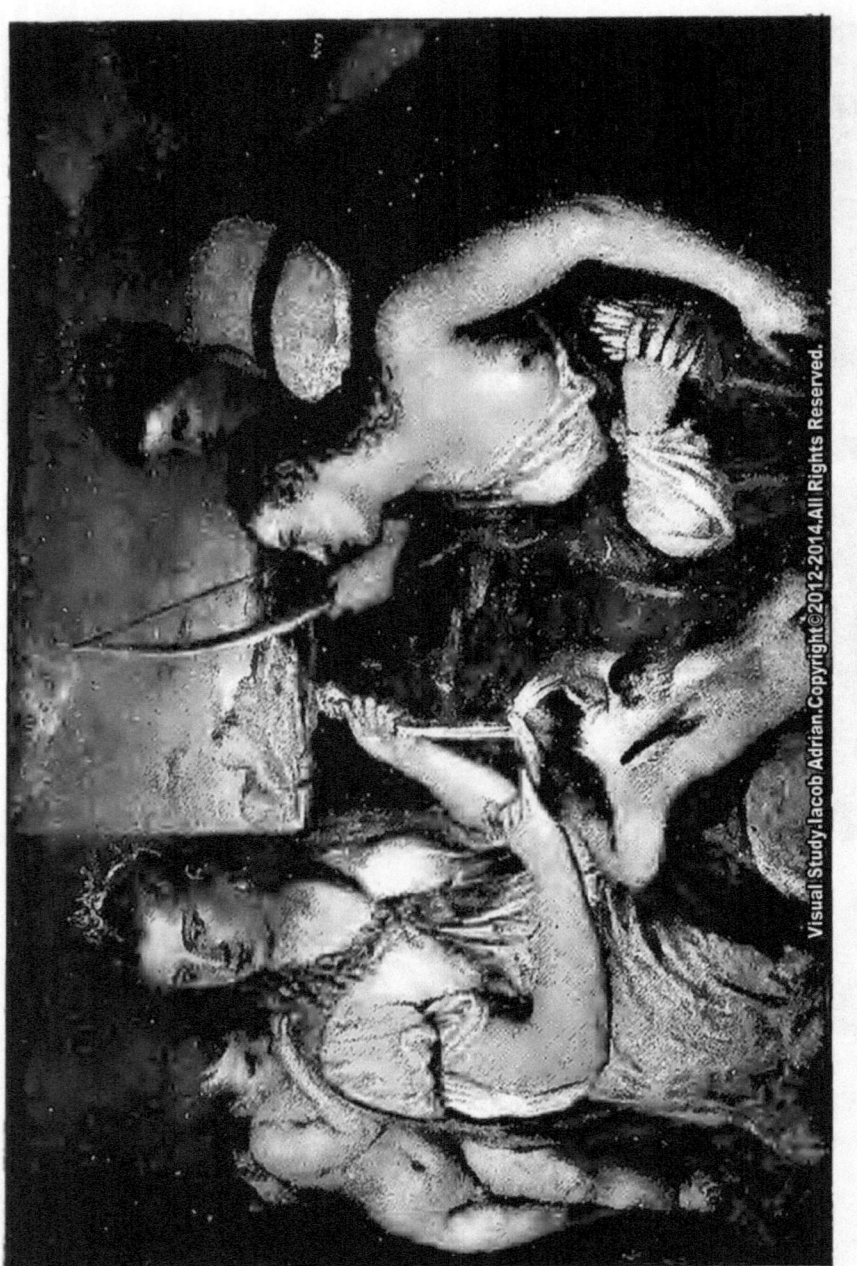

THE EDUCATION OF CUPID
(*Borghese Gallery, Rome*)

DIE ERZIEHUNG DES AMOR
(*Rom, Galerie Borghese*)
F. Hanfstaengl, Photo.

L'ÉDUCATION DE L'AMOUR
(*Galerie Borghèse, Rome*)

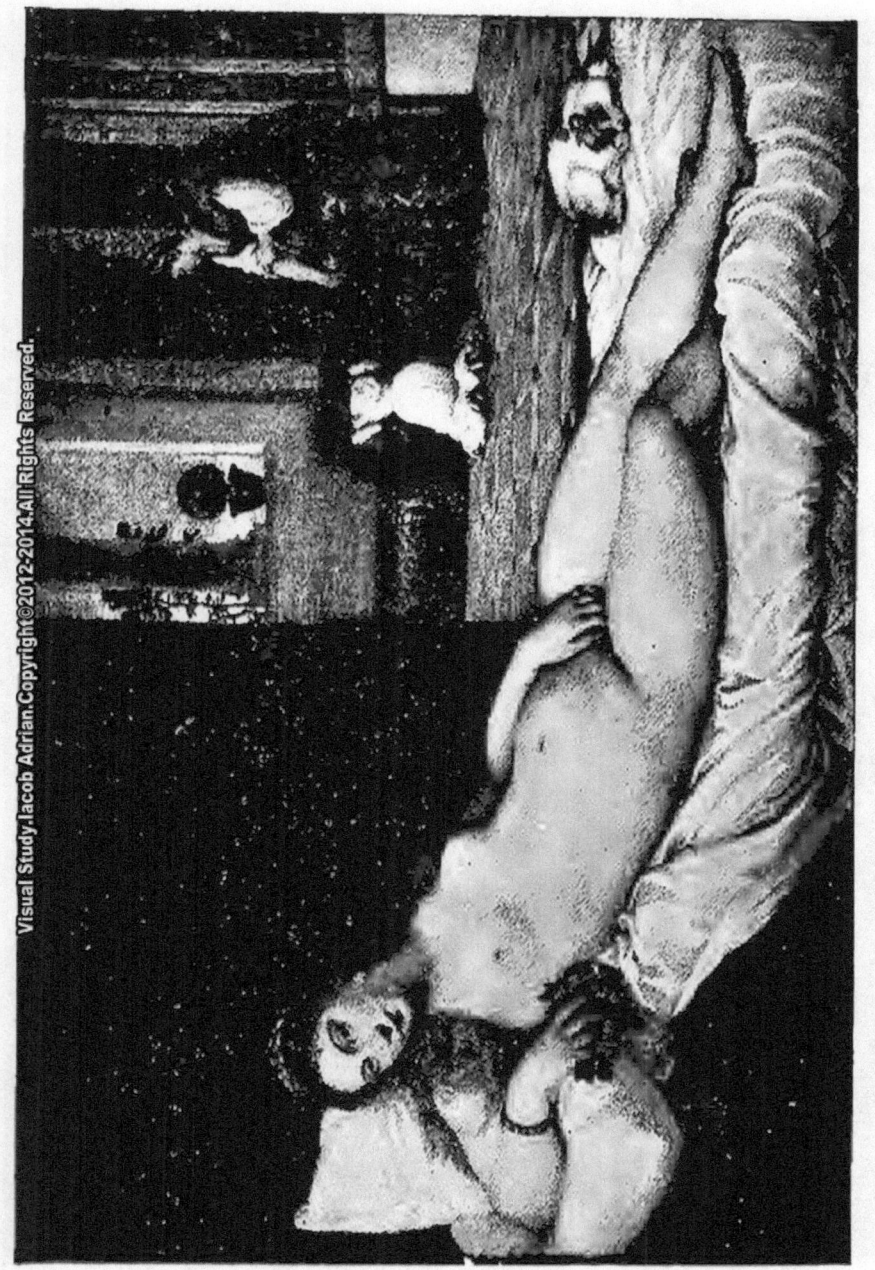

VENUS RECLINING
(Uffizi, Florence)

RUHENDE VENUS
(Florenz, Uffizien)
F. Hanfstaengl, Photo.

VÉNUS COUCHÉE
(Galerie des Uffizi, Florence)

34

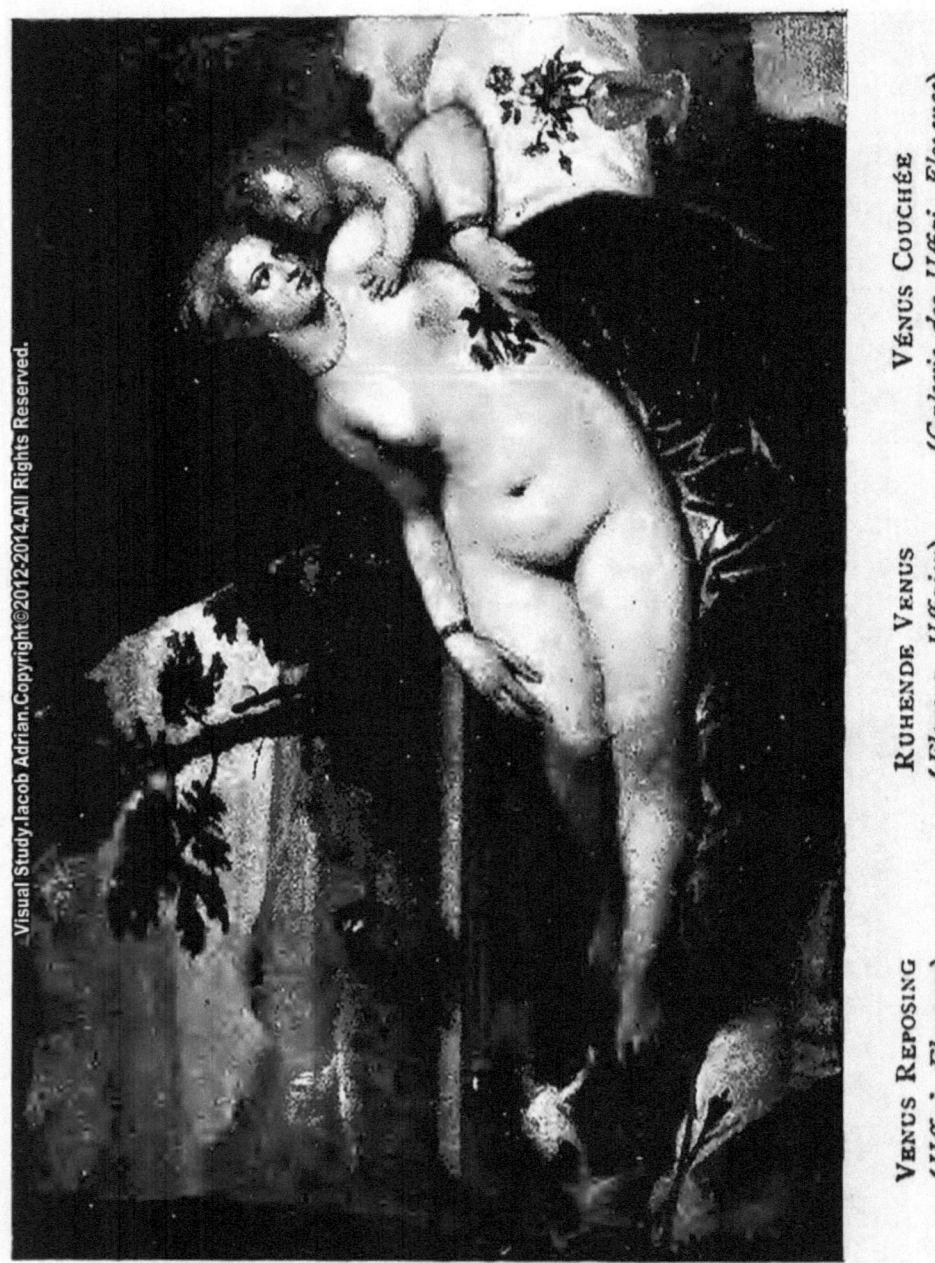

VENUS REPOSING
(Uffizi, Florence)

RUHENDE VENUS
(Florenz, Uffizien)
F. Hanfstaengl, Photo.

VÉNUS COUCHÉE
(Galerie des Uffizi, Florence)

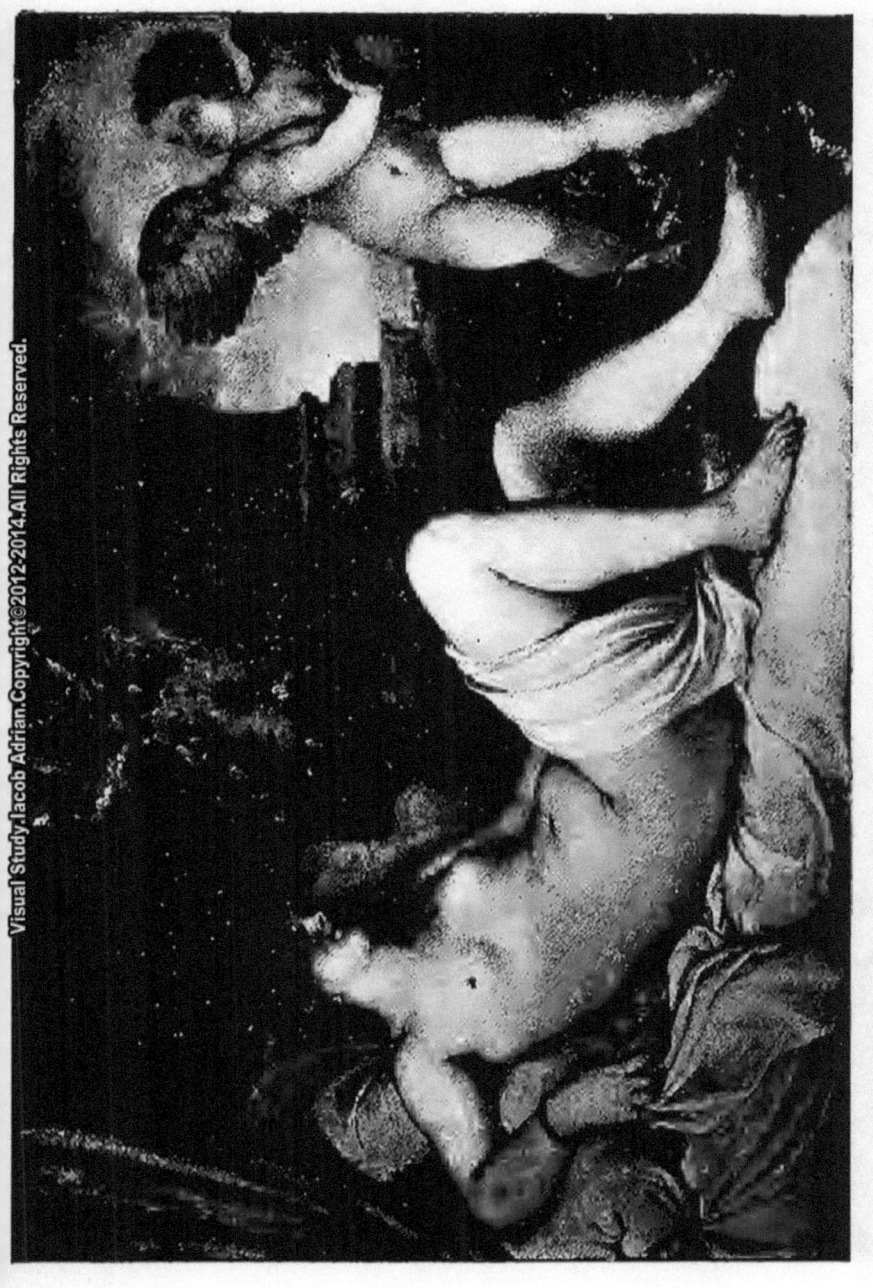

DANAË AND CUPID
(National Museum, Naples)

DANAË
(Neapel, Nationalmuseum)
F. Hanfstaengl, Photo.

DANAÊ
(Musée national, Naples)

36

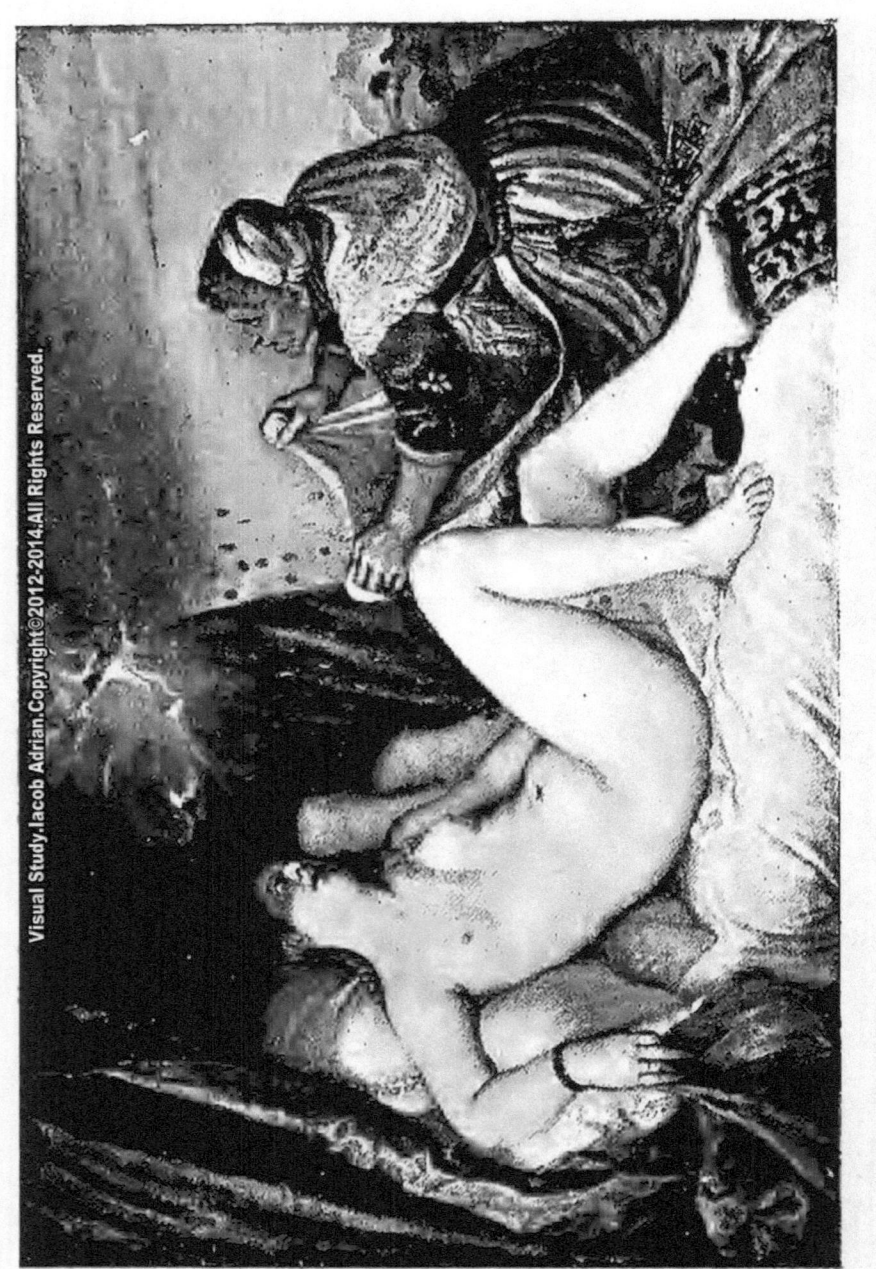

DANAË
(The Hermitage, St. Petersburg)

DANAÉ
(Petersburg, Eremitage)
F. Hanfstaengl, Photo.

DANAÉ
(L'Ermitage, Saint-Pétersbourg)

37

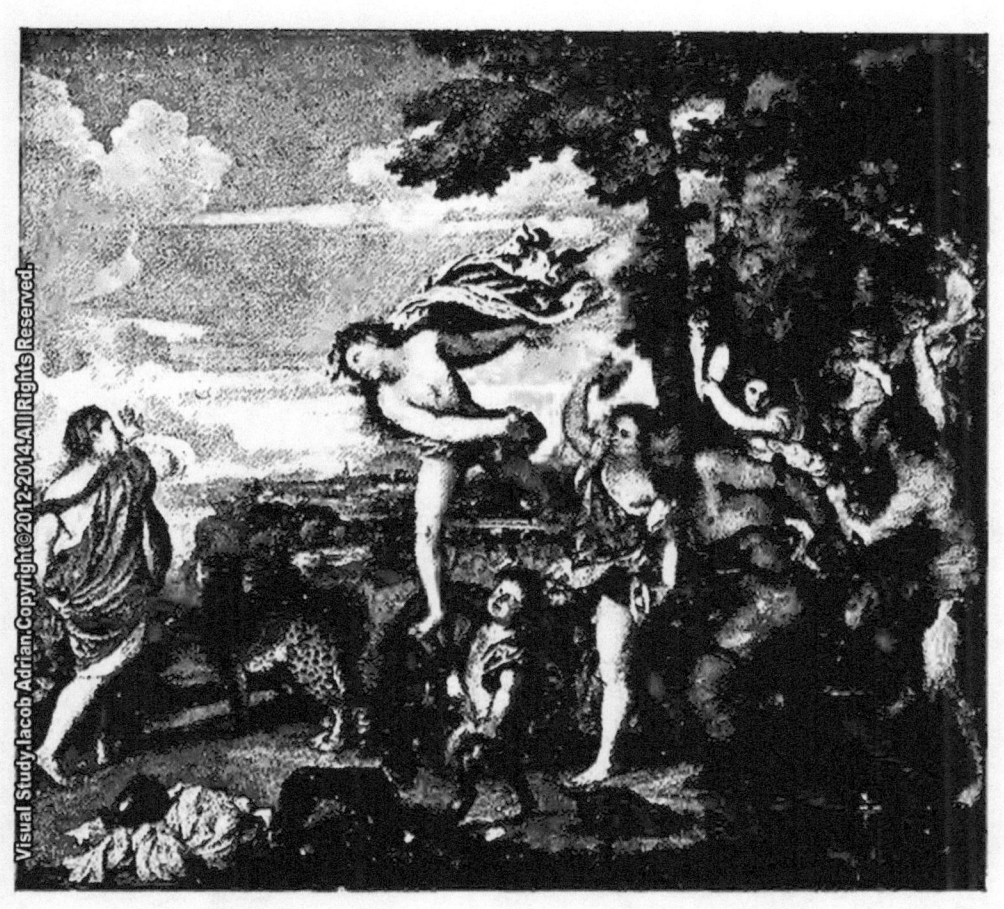

BACCHUS AND ARIADNE
(*National Gallery, London*)
BACCHUS ET ARIADNE
(*Galerie nationale, Londres*)
BACCHUS UND ARIADNE
(*London, Nationalgalerie*)
F. Hanfstaengl, Photo.

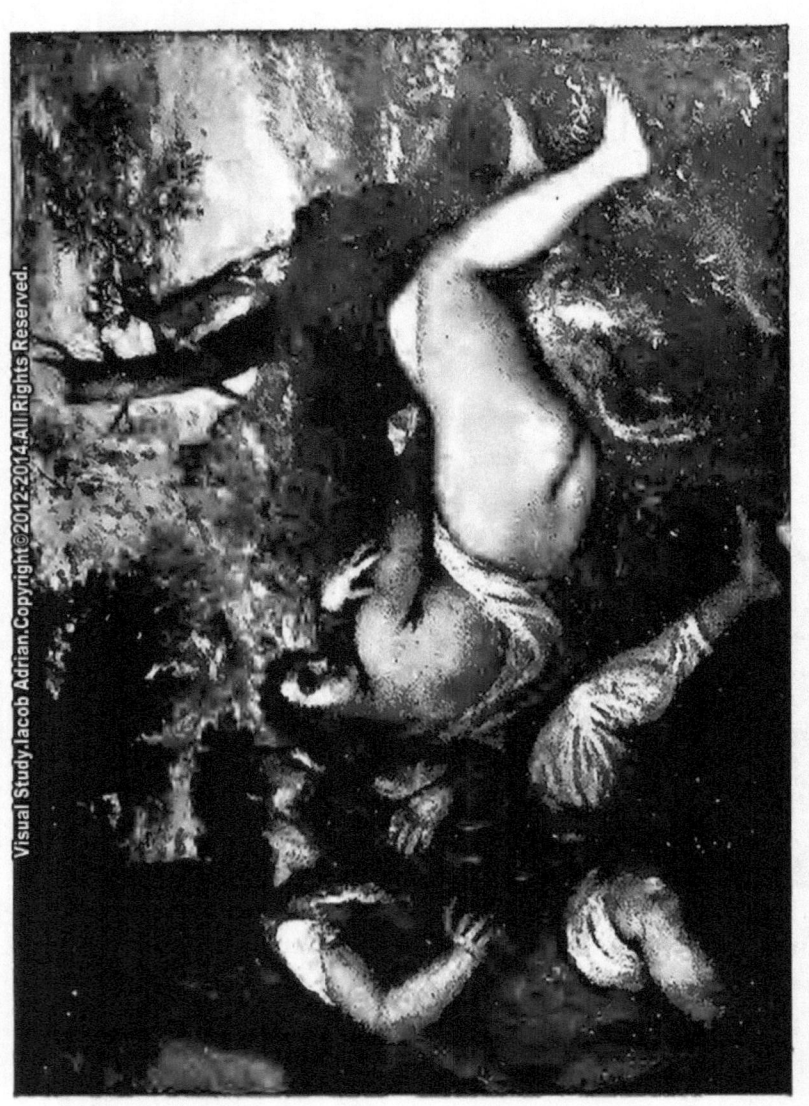

NYMPH AND SHEPHERD
(*Imperial Gallery, Vienna*)

NYMPHE UND SCHÄFER
(*Wien, Kaiserl. Galerie*)
F. Hanfstaengl, Photo.

NYMPHE ET BERGER
(*Galerie impériale, Vienne*)

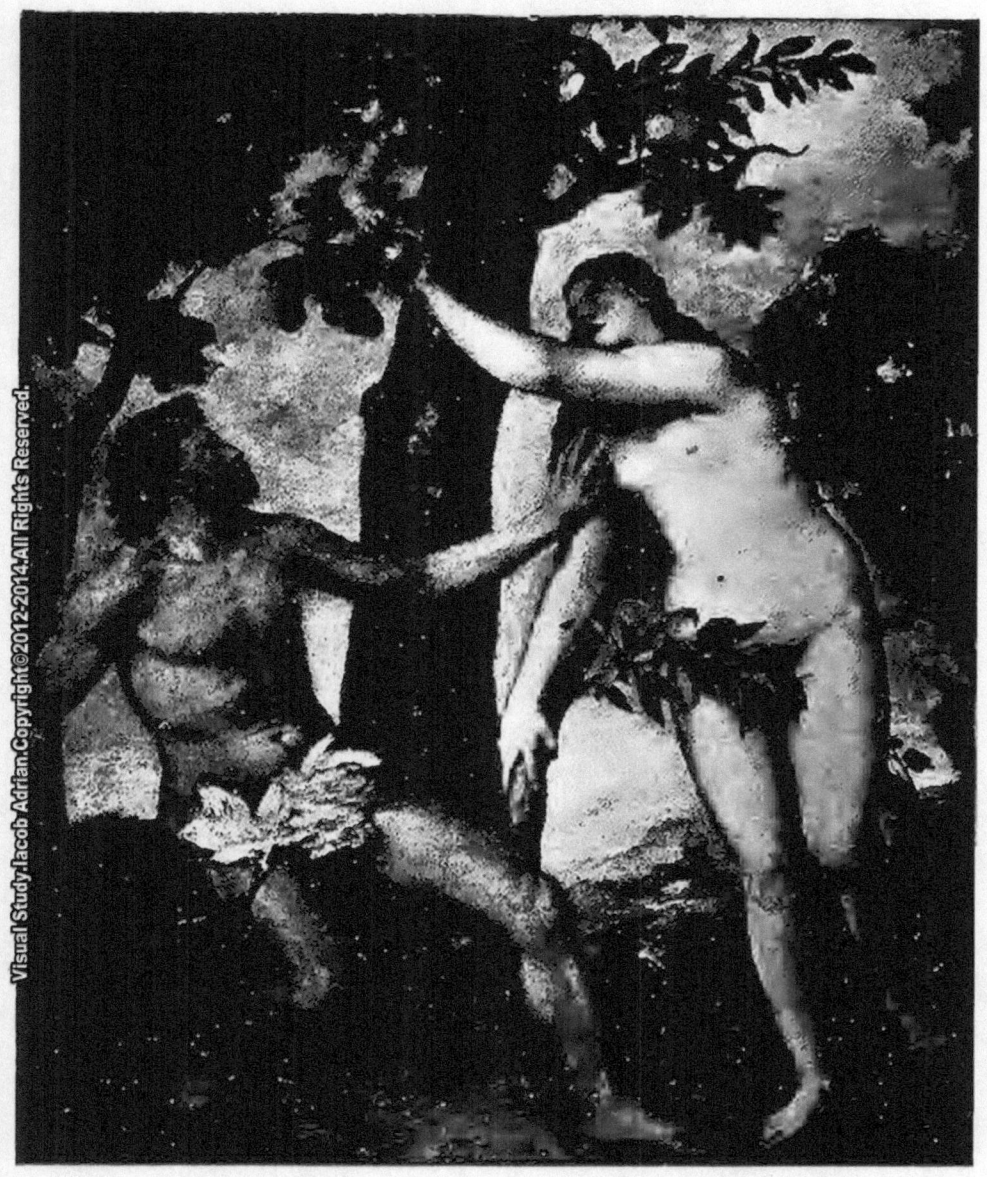

THE FALL OF MAN   LE PÉCHÉ ORIGINEL
(Prado, Madrid)   *(Prado, Madrid)*

DER SÜNDENFALL
(Madrid, Prado)
Braun, Clément & Co., Photo.

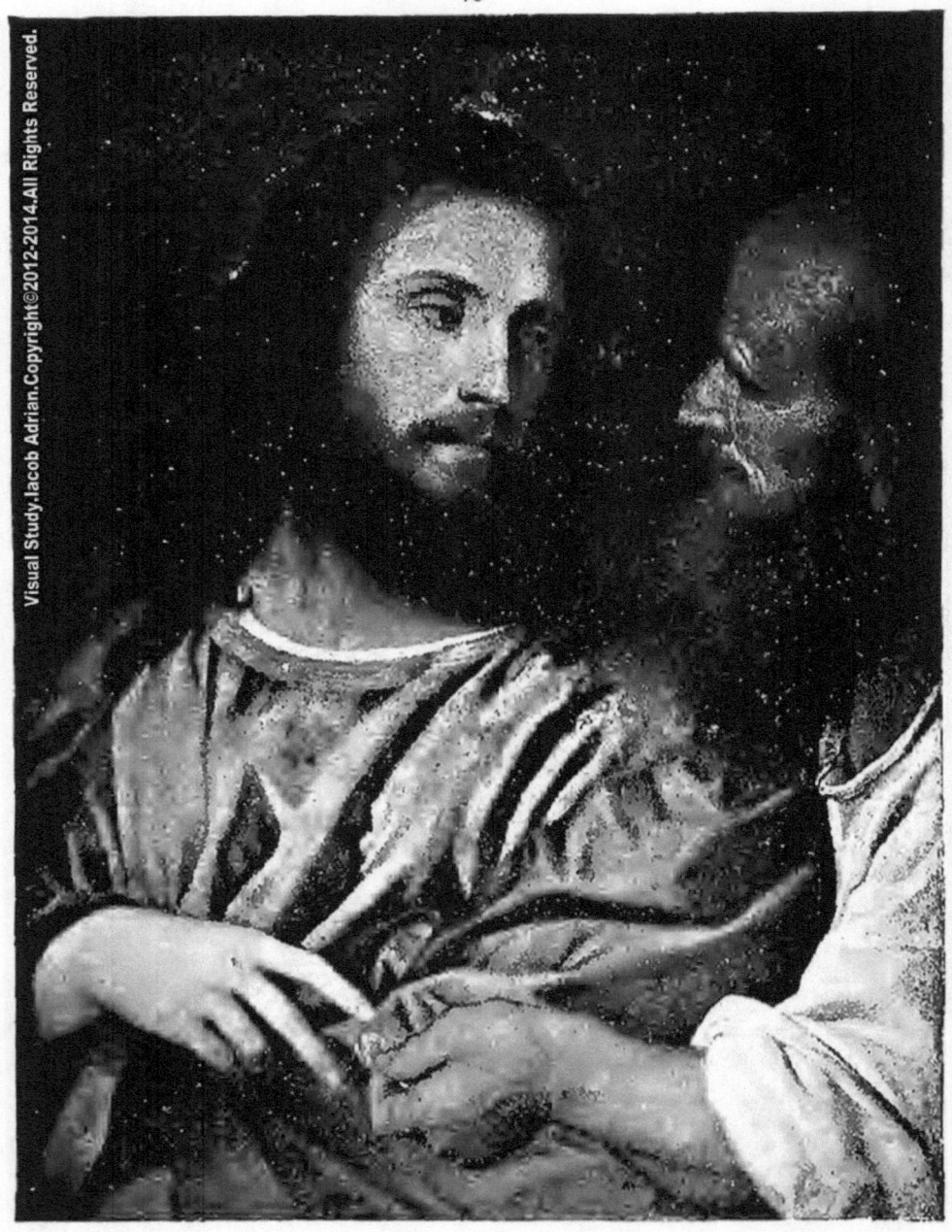

THE TRIBUTE MONEY   LE CHRIST À LA MONNAIE
(*Royal Gallery, Dresden*)   (*Galerie royale, Dresde*)
DER ZINSGROSCHEN
(*Dresden, Kgl. Galerie*)
F. Hanfstaengl, Photo.

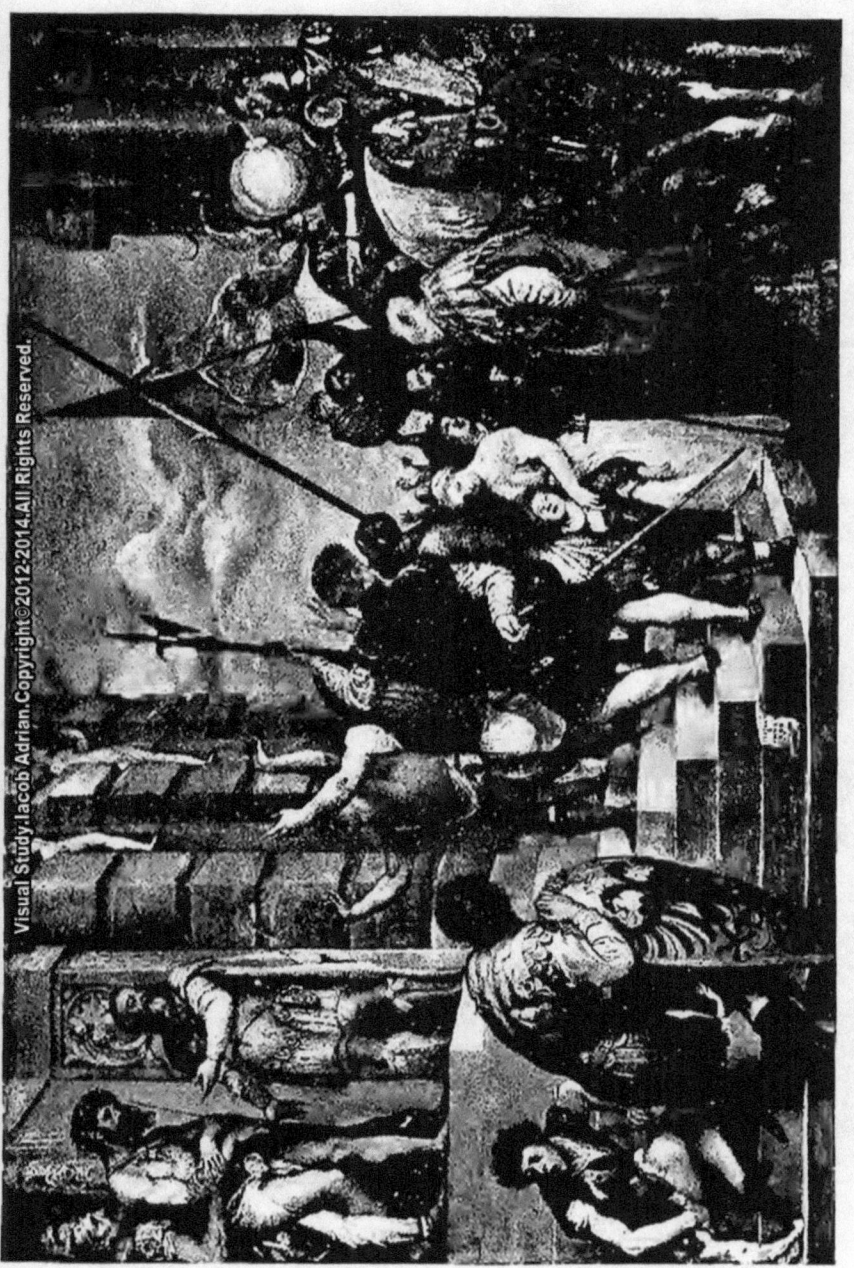

ECCE HOMO
(Imperial Gallery, Vienna)

ECCE HOMO
(Wien, Kaiserl. Galerie)
F. Hanfstaengl, Photo.

ECCE HOMO
(Galerie impériale, Vienne)

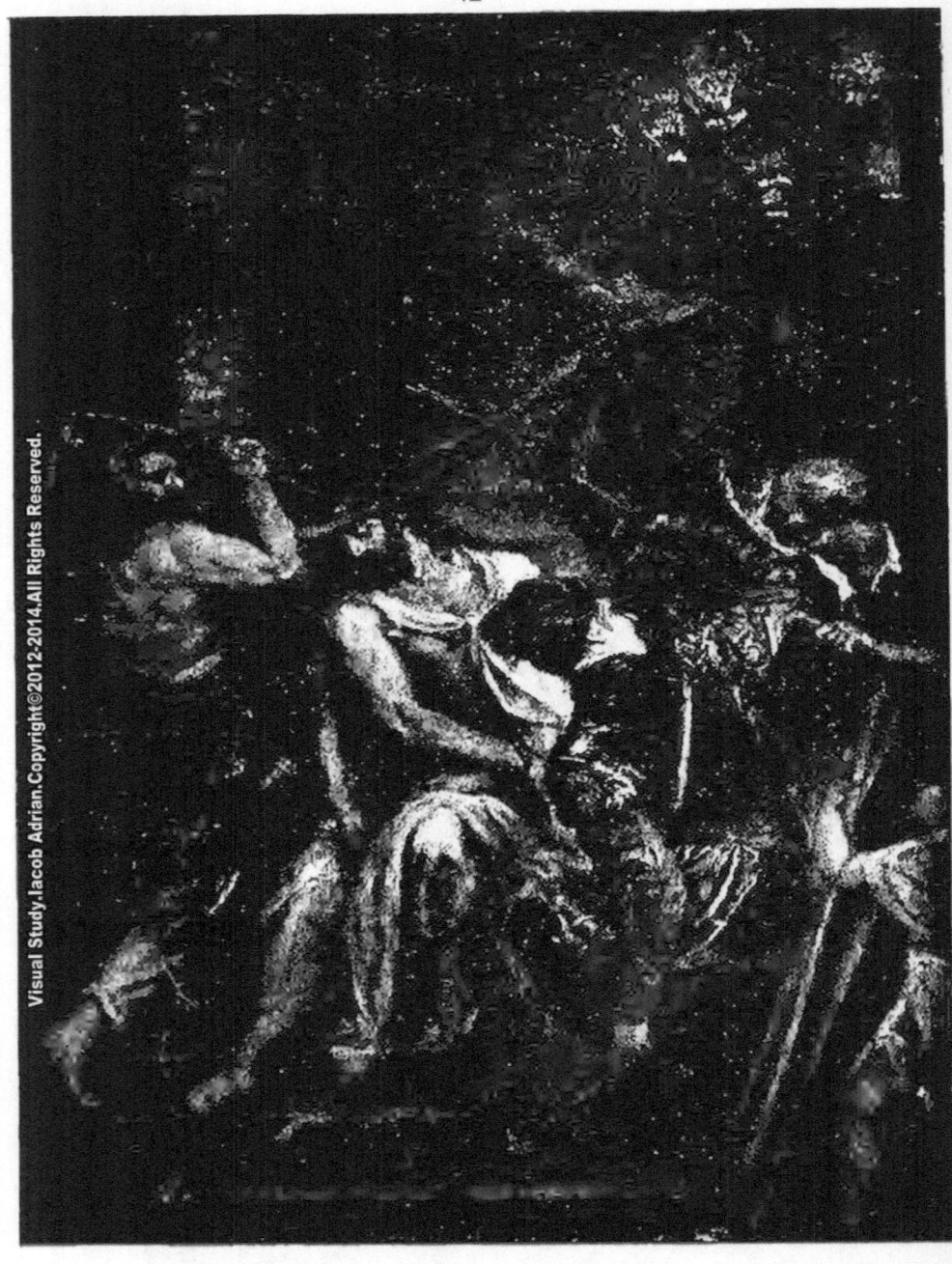

CHRIST CROWNED WITH THORNS   LE COURONNEMENT D'ÉPINES
(Pinakothek, Munich)   *(Pinacothèque, Munich)*
DIE DORNENKRÖNUNG CHRISTI
(München, Pinakothek)
F. Hanfstaengl, Photo.

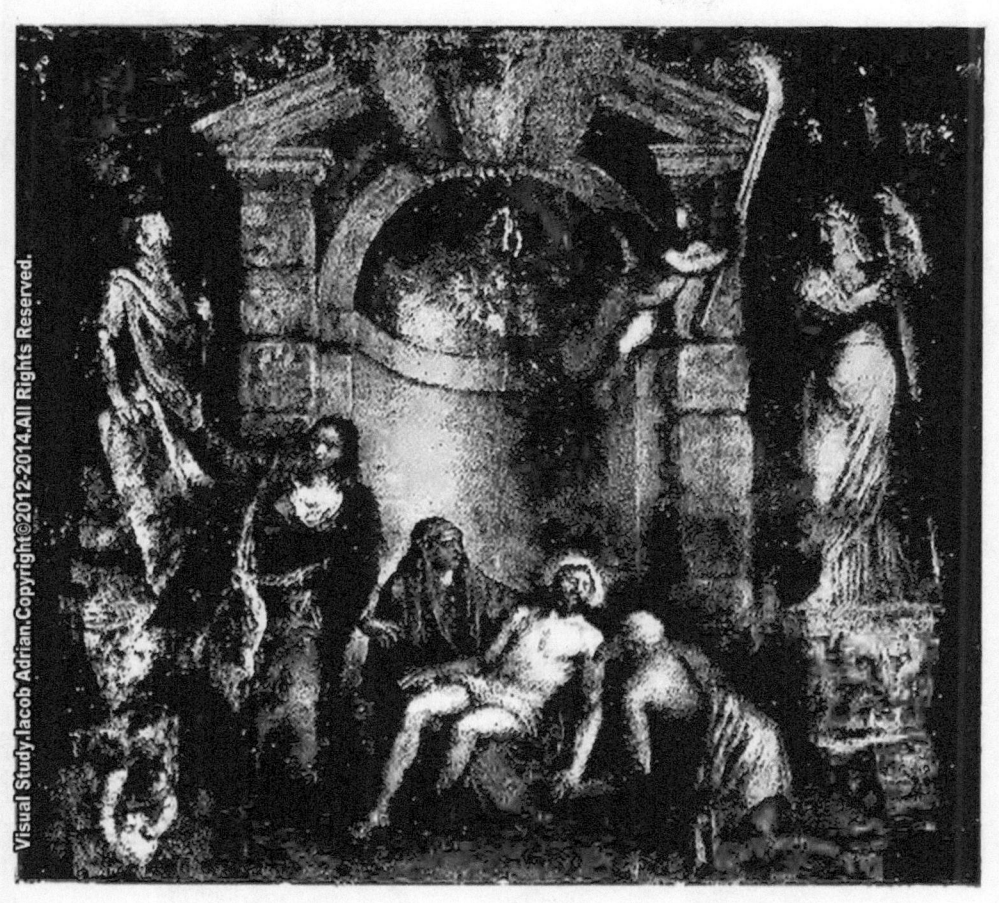

THE DEPOSITION
(*Academy, Venice*)

LA DESCENTE DE CROIX
(*Academie, Venise*)

DIE KREUZABNAHME
(*Venedig, Akademie*)
F. Hanfstaengl, Photo.

44

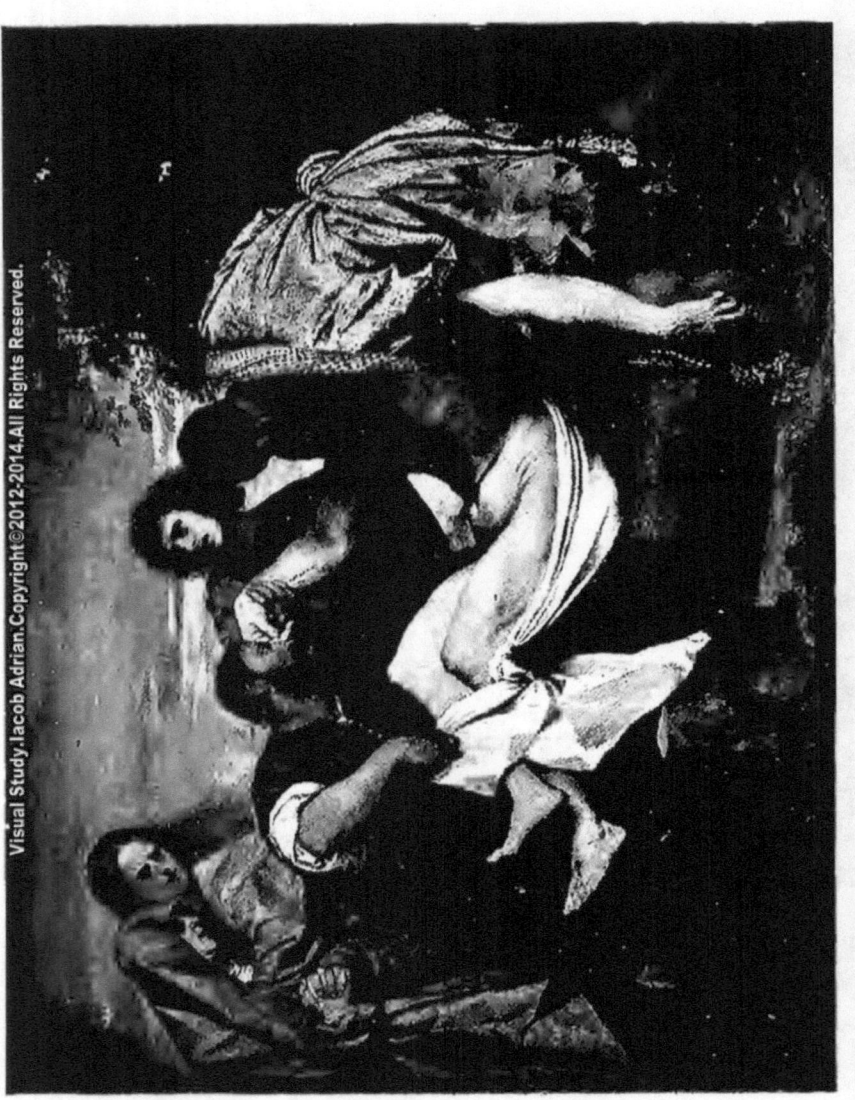

THE ENTOMBMENT
(*Louvre, Paris*)

DIE GRABLEGUNG CHRISTI
(*Paris, Louvre*)

LA MISE AU TOMBEAU
(*Louvre, Paris*)

Braun, Clément & Co., Photo.

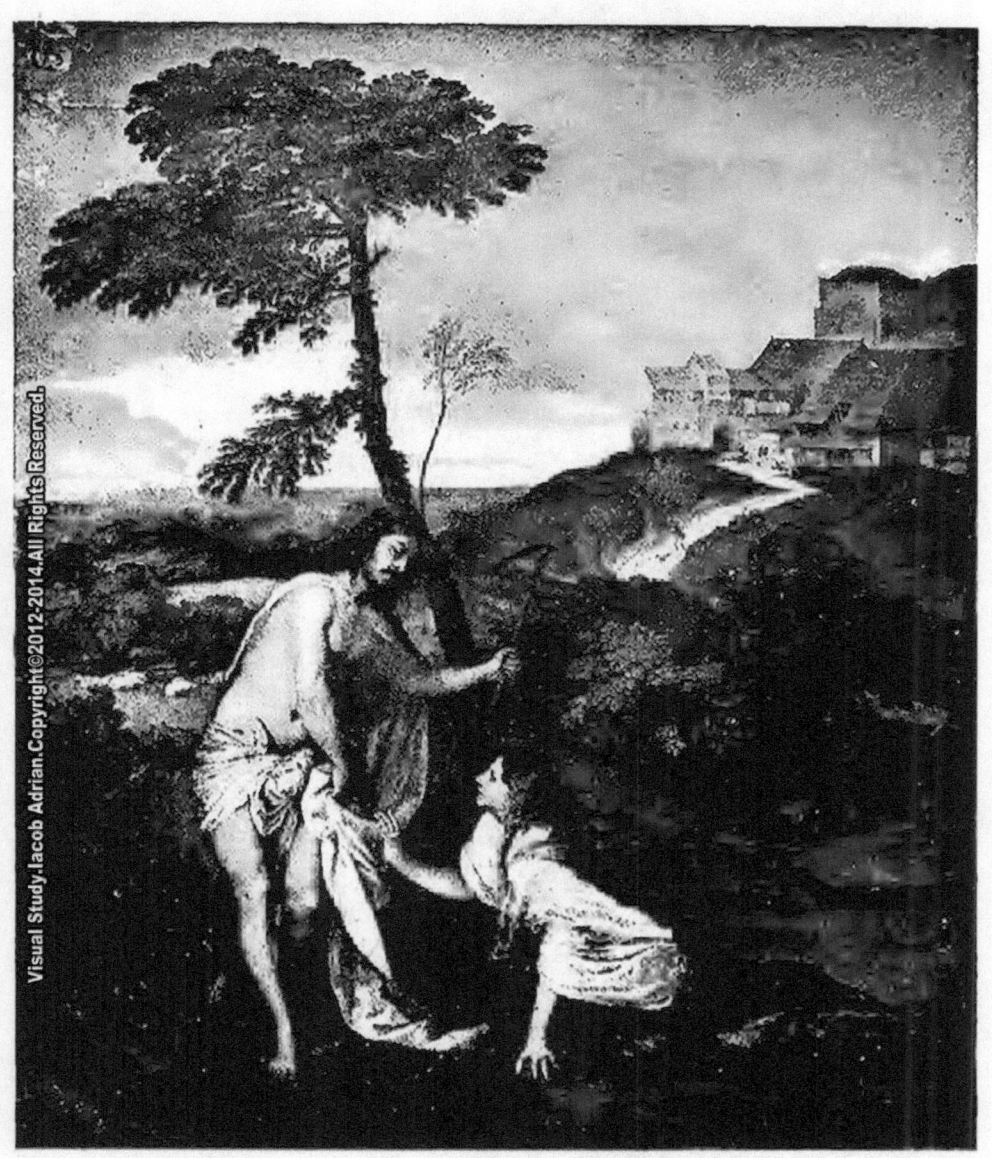

NOLI ME TANGERE
(*National Gallery, London*)

NOLI ME TANGERE
(*Galerie nationale, Londres*)

NOLI ME TANGERE
(*London, Nationalgalerie*)
F. Hanfstaengl, Photo.

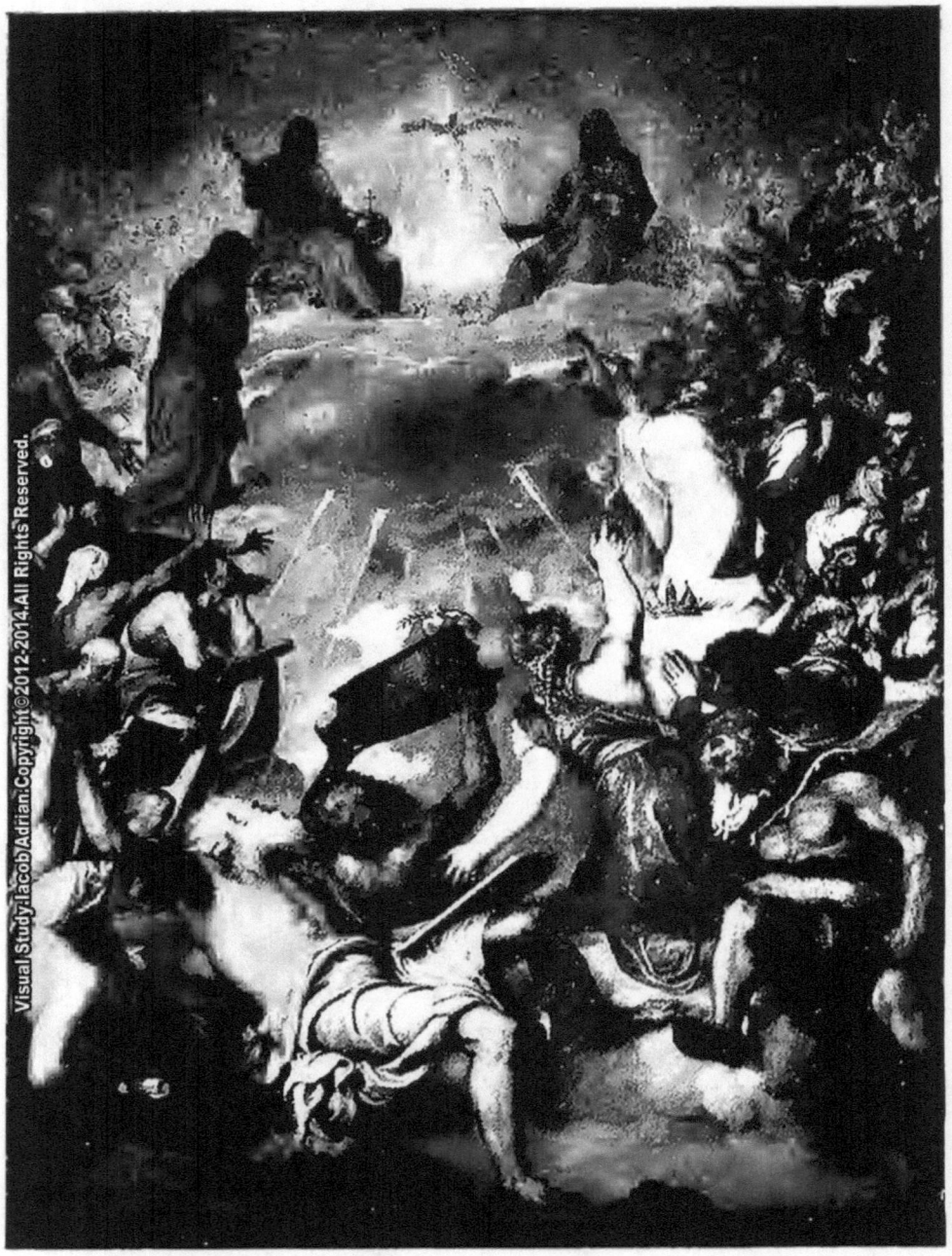

THE HOLY TRINITY   LA SAINTE TRINITÉ
(*Prado, Madrid*)   (*Prado, Madrid*)
DIE HEILIGE DREIFALTIGKEIT
(*Madrid, Prado*)
Braun, Clément & Co., Photo.

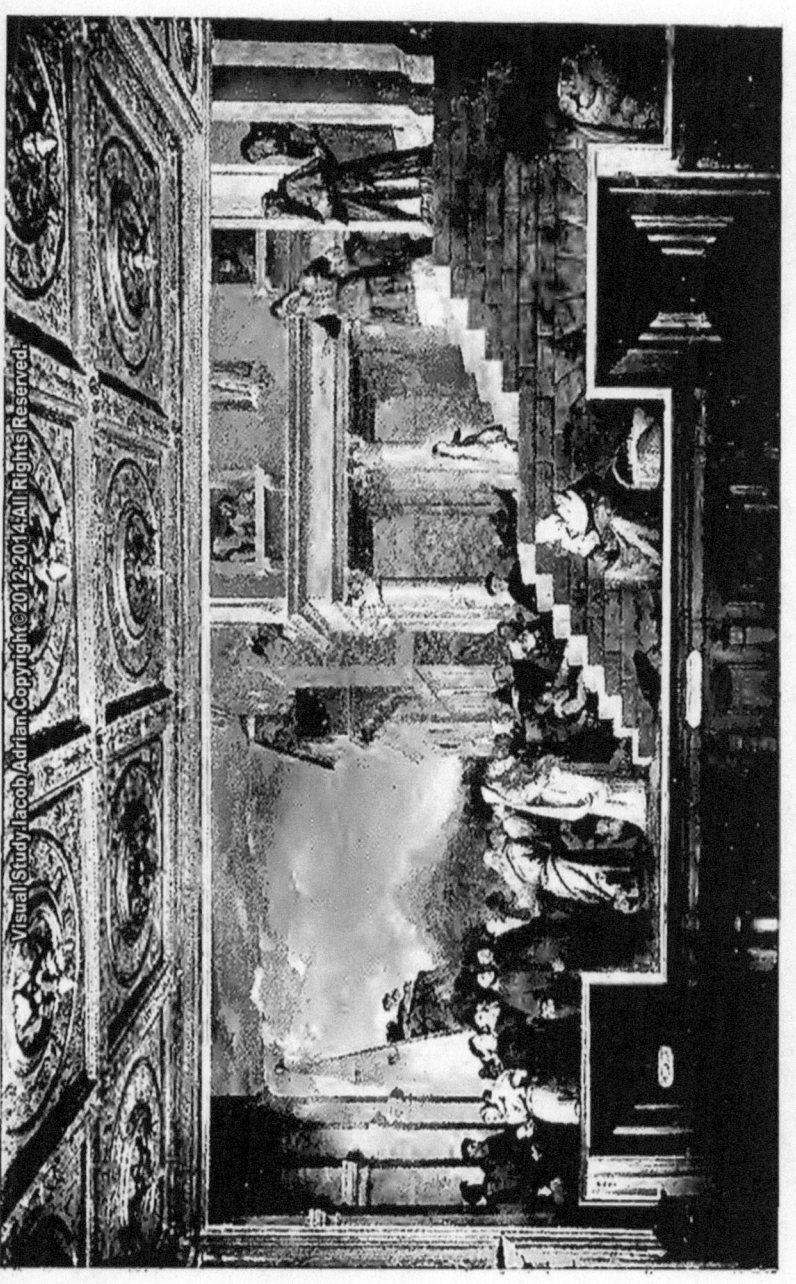

The Presentation of the Virgin
(*Academy, Venice*)

La Présentation de la Vierge
(*Academie, Venise*)

Die Darstellung der Maria
(*Venedig, Akademie*)

F. Hanfstaengl, Photo.

48

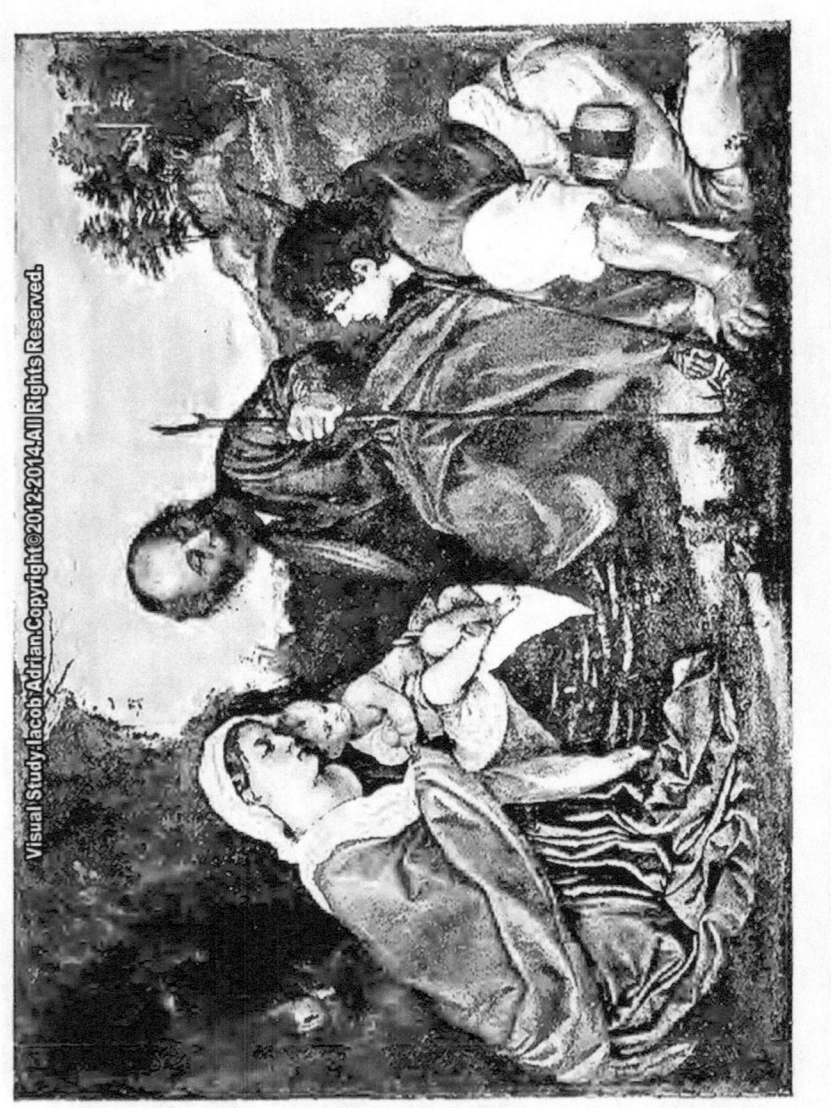

THE HOLY FAMILY
(*National Gallery, London*)

LA SAINTE FAMILLE
(*Galerie nationale, Londres*)

DIE HEILIGE FAMILIE
(*London, Nationalgalerie*)
F. Hanfstaengl, Photo.

49

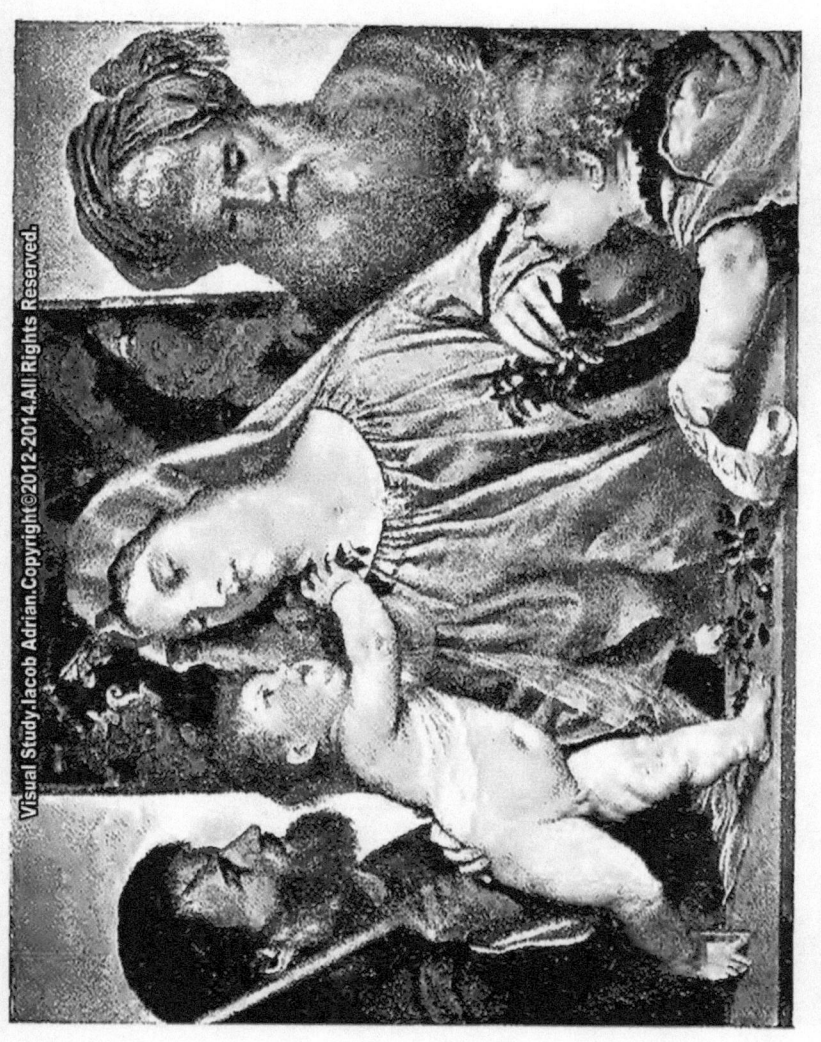

THE "CHERRY" MADONNA   LA VIERGE AUX CERISES
(Imperial Gallery, Vienna)   (Galerie impériale, Vienne)
DIE KIRSCHEN-MADONNA
(Wien, Kaiserl. Galerie)
F. Hanfstaengl, Photo.

50

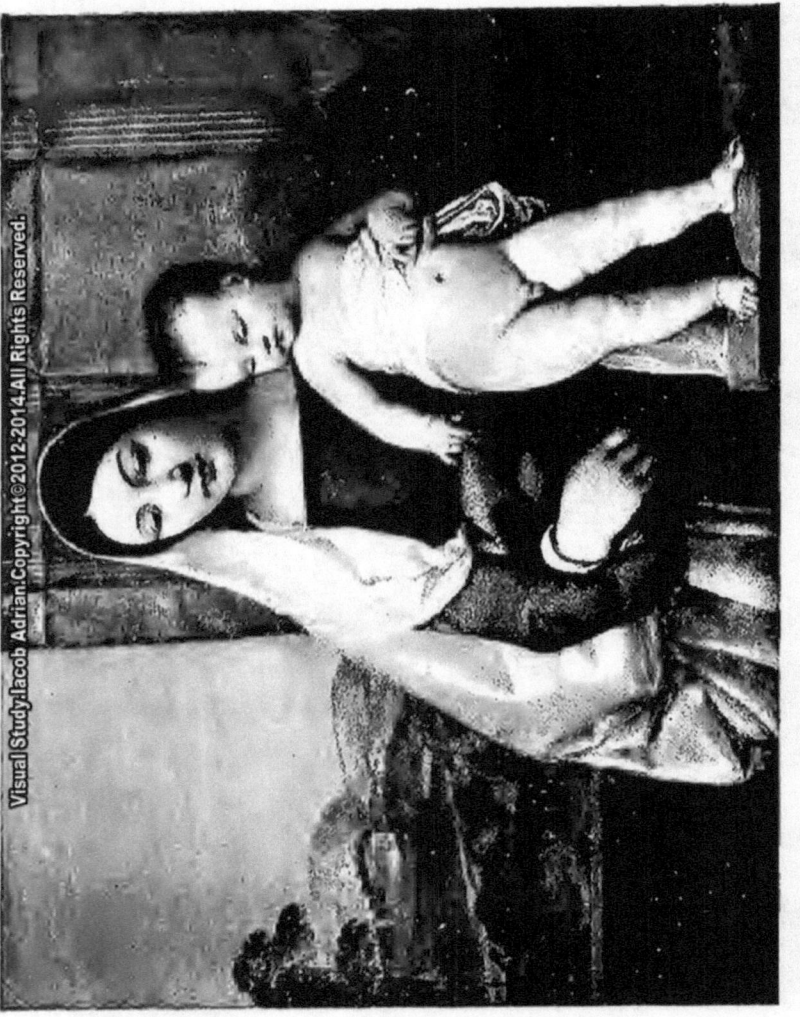

THE "GIPSY" MADONNA
(*Imperial Gallery, Vienna*)

DIE ZIGEUNER-MADONNA
(*Wien, Kaiserl. Galerie*)

LA VIERGE ET L'ENFANT
(*Galerie impériale, Vienne*)

F. Hanfstaengl, Photo.

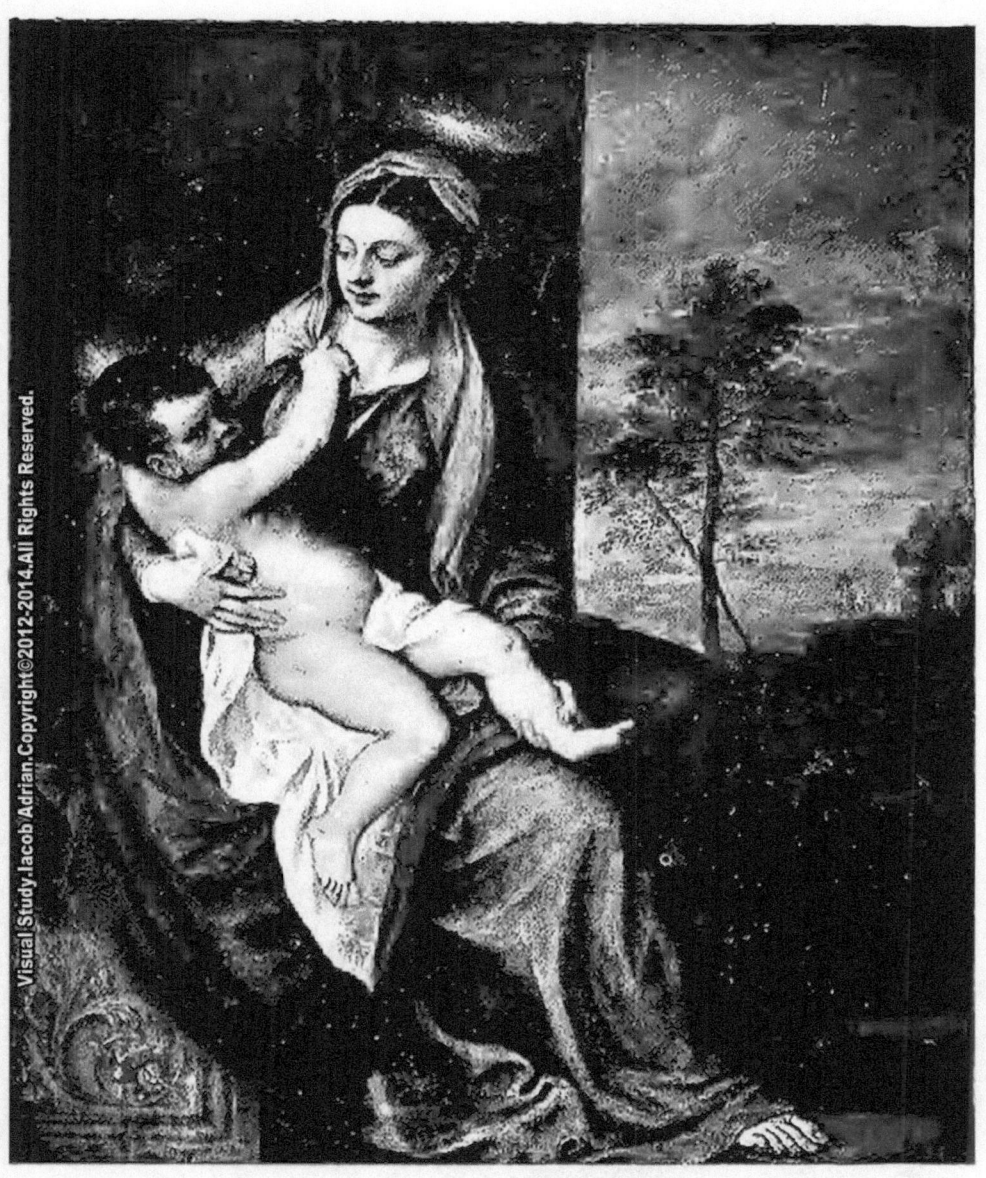

THE VIRGIN AND CHILD   LA VIERGE ET L'ENFANT
(Pinakothek, Munich)   *(Pinacothèque, Munich)*
MARIA MIT DEM KINDE
(München, Pinakothek)
F. Hanfstaengl, Photo.

52

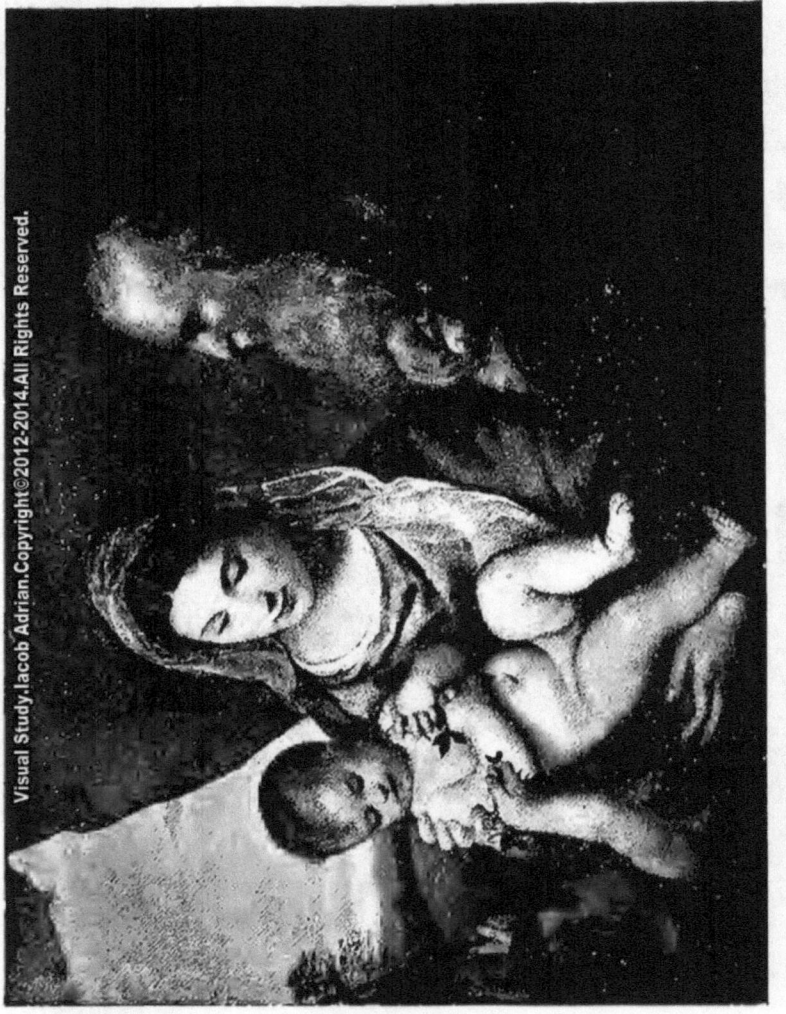

THE VIRGIN AND CHILD,
ST. ANTHONY AND ST. JOHN
(Uffizi, Florence)

LA VIERGE ET L'ENFANT
AVEC ST. ANTOINE ET ST. JEAN
(Galerie des Uffizi, Florence)
MARIA MIT DEM KINDE, DEM KL. JOHANNES UND ST. ANTONIUS
(Florenz, Uffizien)
F. Hanfstaengl, Photo.

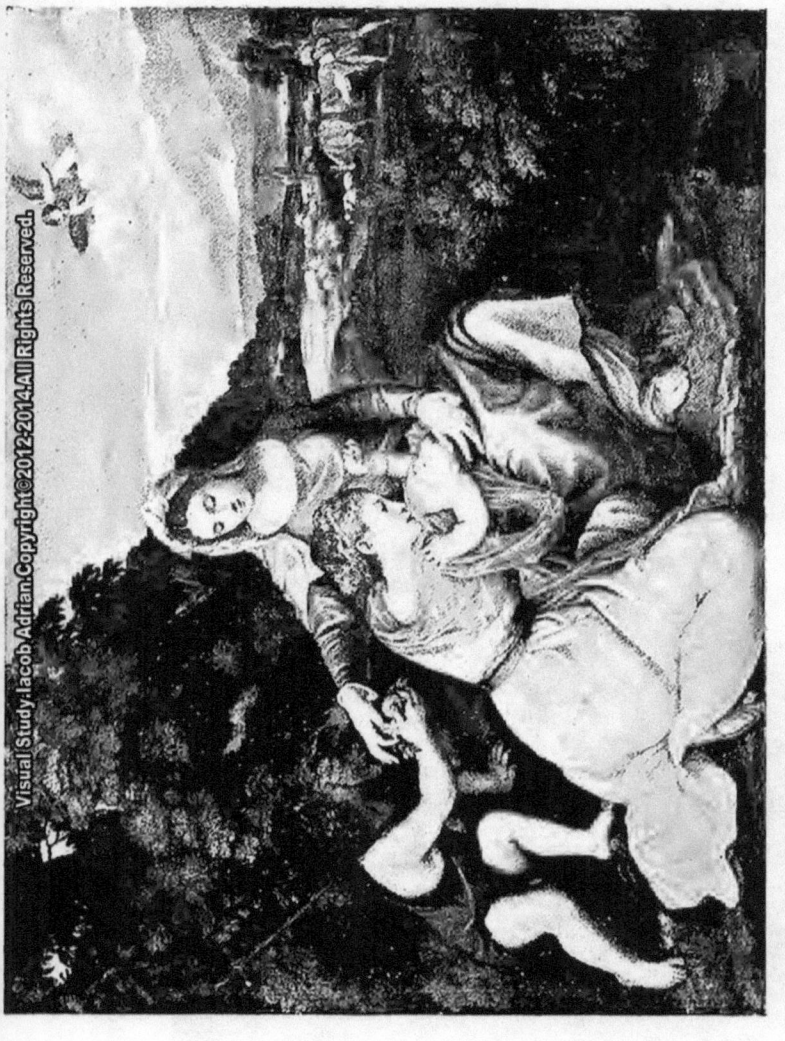

THE VIRGIN AND CHILD,   LA VIERGE ET L'ENFANT,
ST. CATHERINE AND JOHN THE BAPTIST   AVEC ST. JEAN-BAPTISTE ET STE. CATHERINE
(National Gallery, London)   (Galerie nationale, Londres)
MARIA MIT DEM KINDE, ST. JOHANNES UND ST. KATHARINA
(London, Nationalgalerie)
F. Hanfstaengl, Photo.

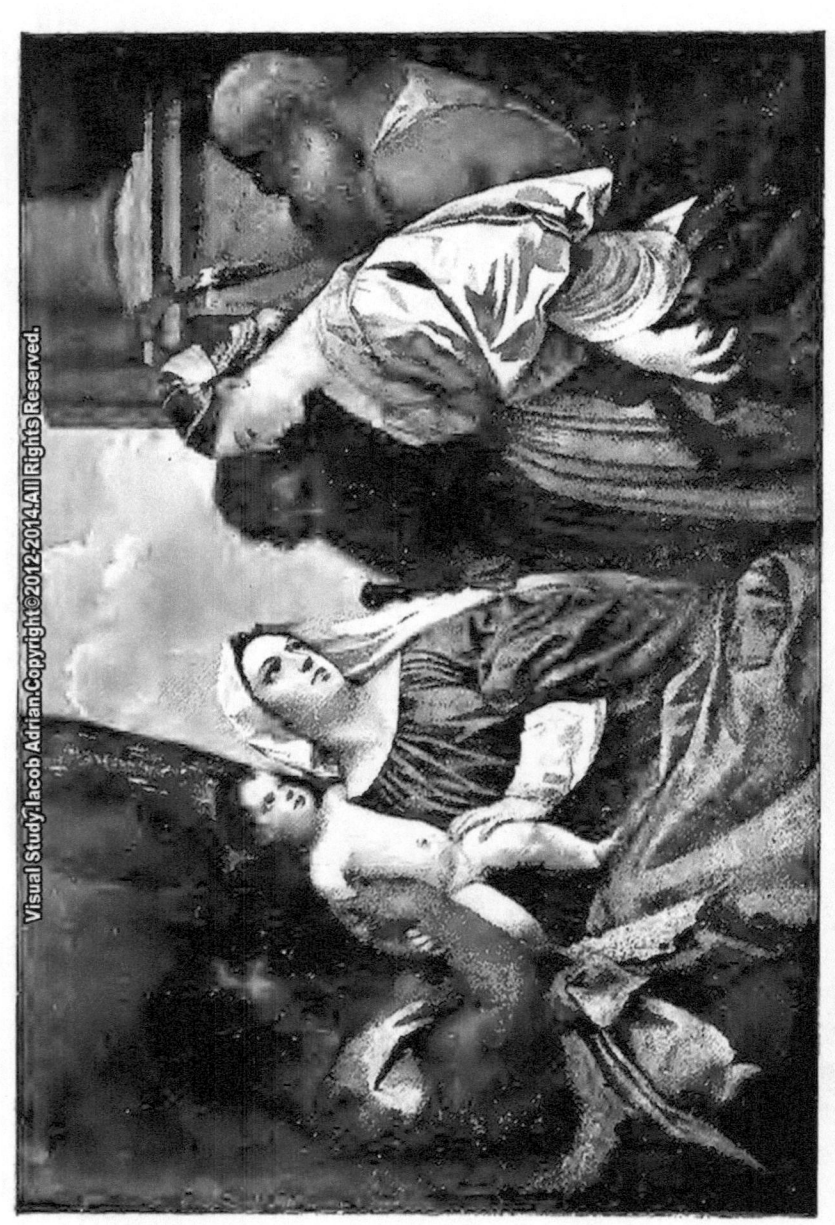

THE VIRGIN AND CHILD
AND FOUR SAINTS
(*Royal Gallery, Dresden*)

MARIA MIT DEM KINDE
UND VIER HEILIGEN
(*Dresden, Kgl. Galerie*)
F. Hanfstaengl, Photo.

LA VIERGE ET L'ENFANT,
AVEC QUATRE SAINTS
(*Galerie royale, Dresde*)

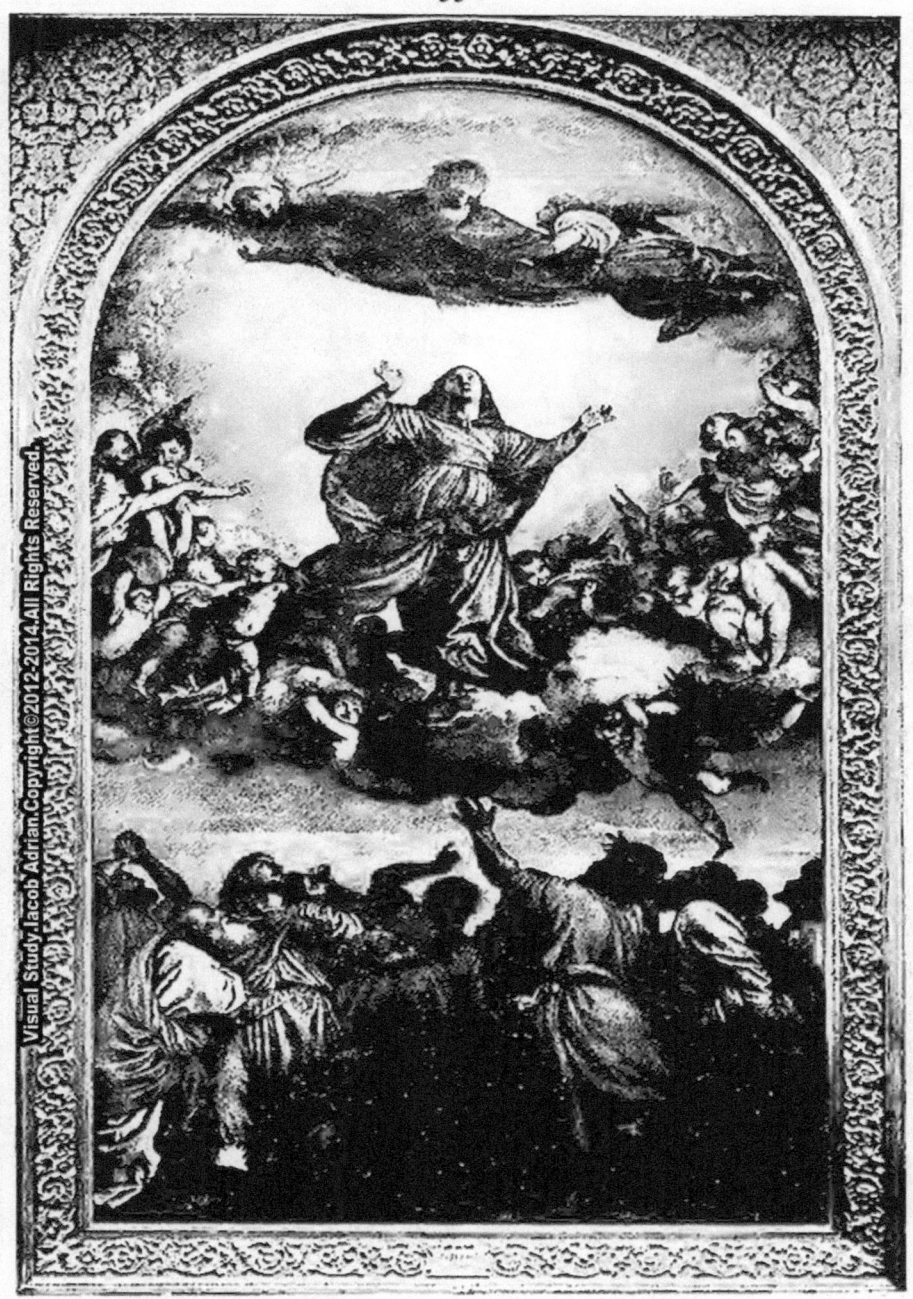

THE ASSUMPTION   L'ASSOMPTION
(Academy, Venice)   *(Académie, Venise)*
MARIÄ HIMMELFAHRT
(Venedig, Academie)
F. Hanfstaengl, Photo.

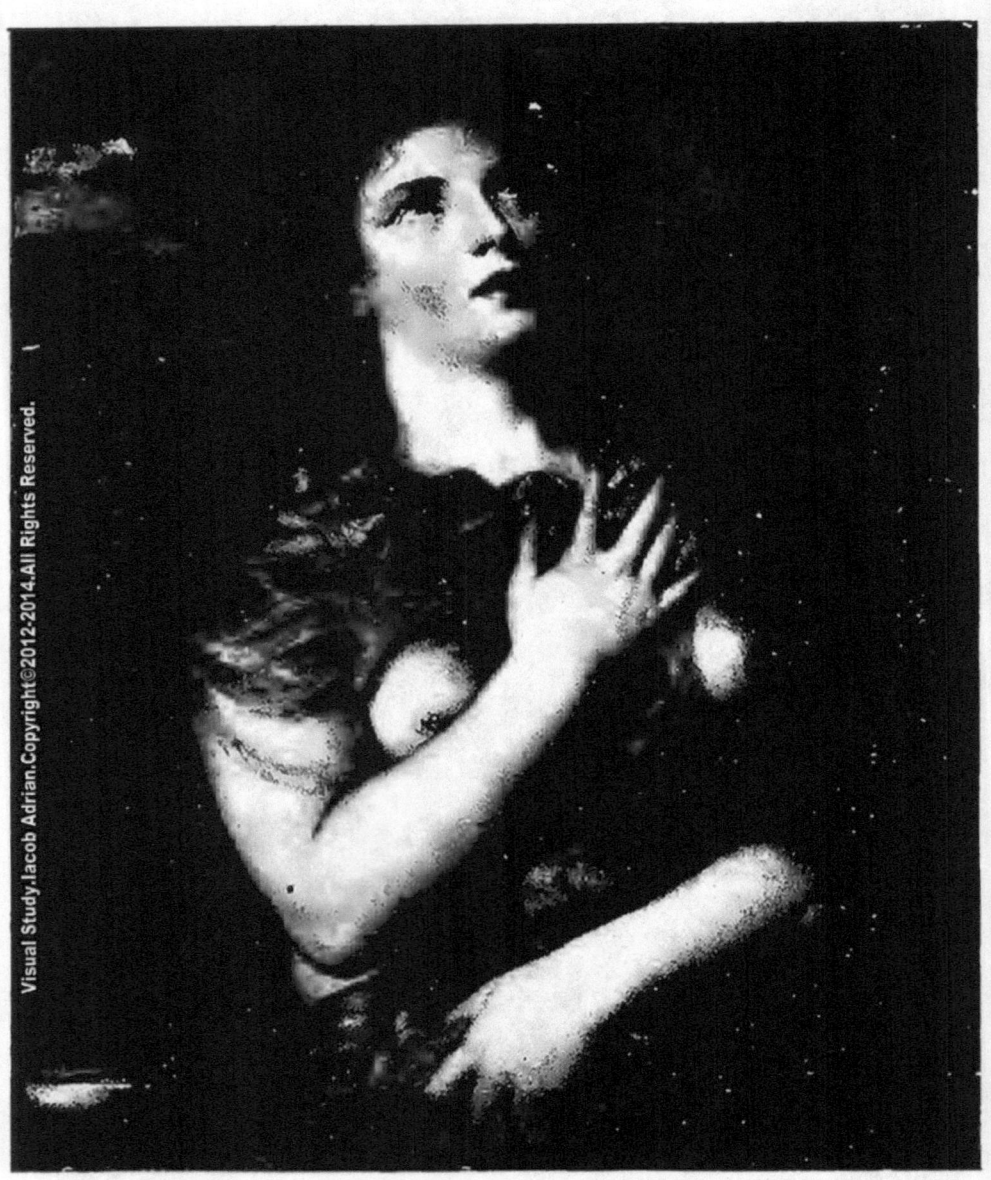

MARY MAGDALENE
(*Pitti, Florence*)

LA MADELEINE
(*Galerie Pitti, Florence*)

ST. MAGDALENA
(*Florenz, Galerie Pitti*)
F. Hanfstaengl, Photo,

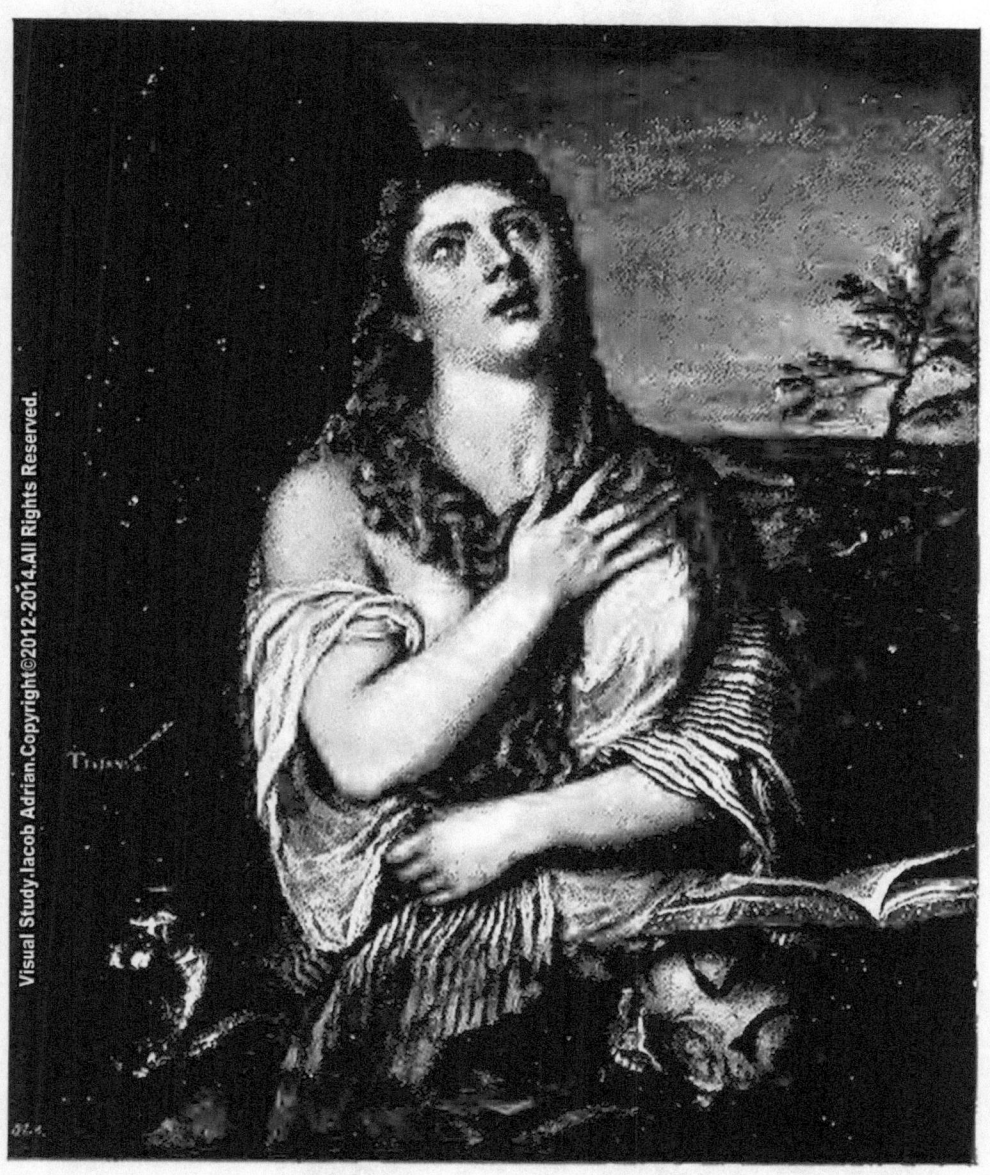

MARY MAGDALENE   LA MADELEINE REPENTANTE
(*The Hermitage, St. Petersburg*)   (*L'Ermitage, Saint-Pétersbourg*)
DIE BÜSSENDE MAGDALENA
(*Petersburg, Eremitage*)
F. Hanfstaengl, Photo.

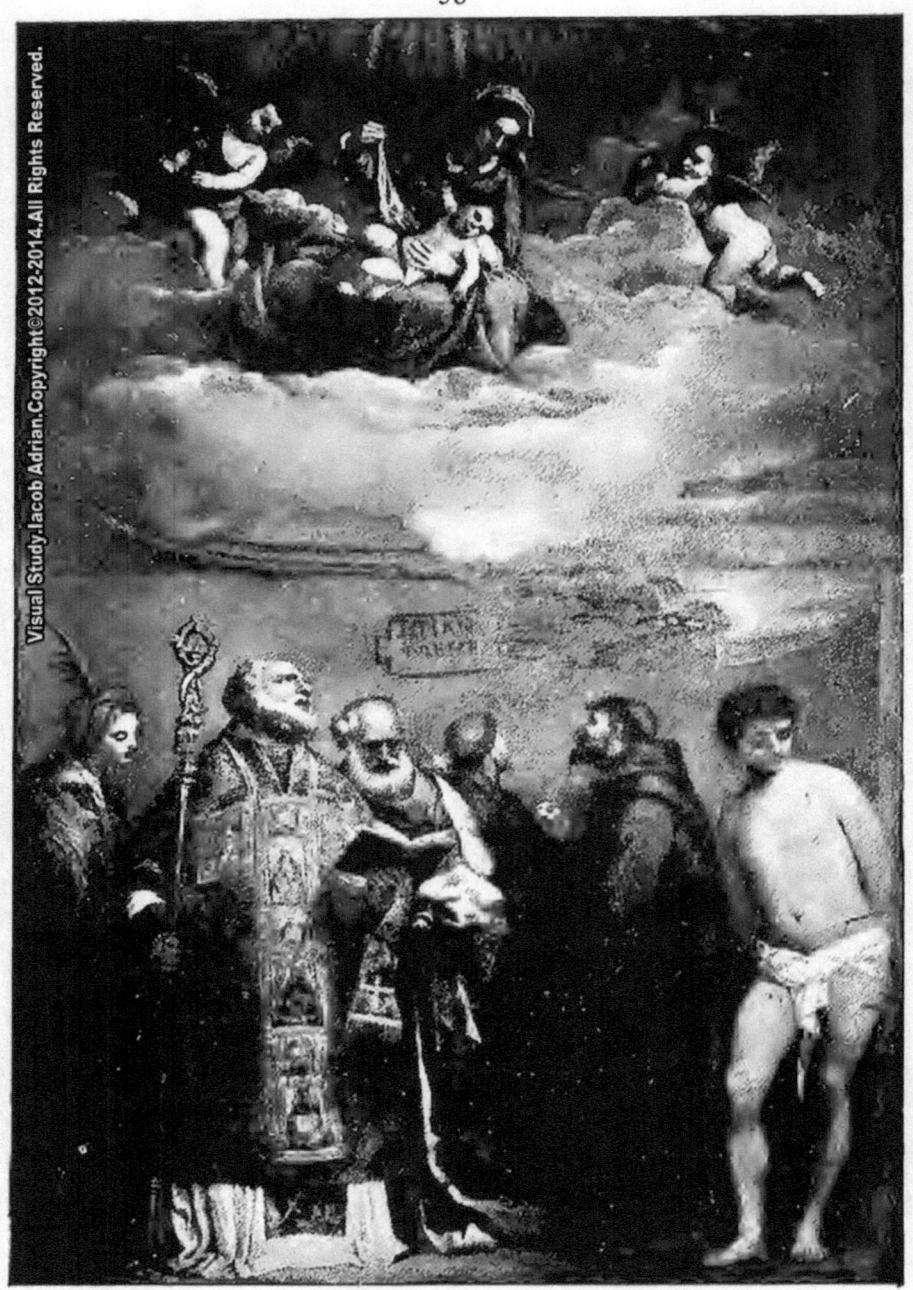

ST. SEBASTIAN
(Vatican, Rome)

ST. SÉBASTIEN
(Vatican, Rome)

ST. SEBASTIAN
(Rom, Vatikan)
F. Hanfstaengl, Photo.

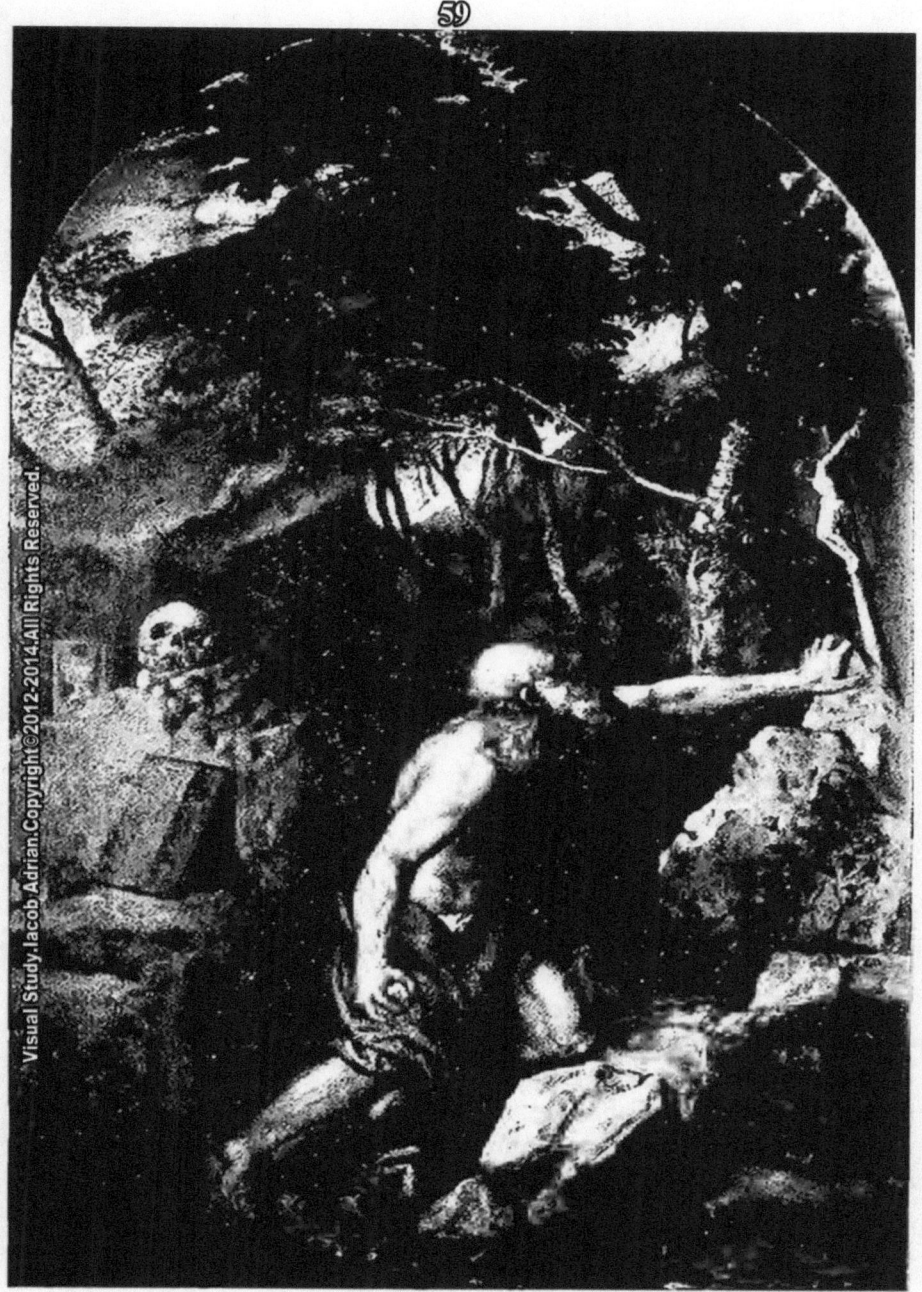

ST. JEROME IN THE
DESERT
(*Brera, Milan*)

ST. JÉRÔME DANS LE
DÉSERT
(*Brera, Milan*)

ST. HIERONYMUS IN DER WÜSTE
(*Milan, Brera*)
F. Hanfstaengl, Photo.

Bibliographic sources :

The masterpieces of Titian (1908)

Author:
Cavagna Sangiuliani di Gualdana, Antonio,
conte, 1843-1913, former owner. IU-R

Publisher: London : Glasgow : Gowans & Gray, Ltd.

This documentary study use,
combined in various proportions,
elements from the following categories,
forms and subsets :
- fair use
- documentary
- documentary photography
- feature
- journalism
- arts journalism
- visual journalism
- photojournalism
- celebrity photography
in order to :
- employ material as the object of cultural critique ,
- quote to illustrate an argument or point ,
- use material in historical sequence,
providing independent opinion,
using photos, press articles, advertisements,
opinions of fans etc. ...